Marilyn, Joe & Me

June DiMaggio Tells It Like It Was

JUNE DIMAGGIO
with
MARY JANE POPP

PENMARIN BOOKS

Editorial Offices
Penmarin Books
1044 Magnolia Way
Roseville, CA 95661
(916) 771-5869

Sales and Customer Service Offices
Midpoint Trade Books
27 West 20th Street, Suite 1102
New York, NY 10011
(212) 727-0190

Penmarin Books are available at special discounts for bulk purchases for premiums, sales promotions, or education. For details, contact the publisher. On your letterhead, include information regarding the intended use of the book and how many you wish to purchase.

During the preparation of this manuscript every effort has been made to obtain all appropriate permissions for each photograph. If superior rights to such photographs do exist, those individuals who prepared this manucript sincerely regret such errors and will take the necessary steps to correct the errors and make sure that such errors do not appear in future editions of this manuscript.

ISBN 1-883955-63-7

Cover design by the Dunlavey Studio and Vanessa Perez.
Text design by The Cowans

Printed in the United States of America.

Library of Congress number: 2006933515

DEDICATION

To my beautiful soul mate, friend, voice teacher,
minister, mentor, metaphysician,
and celebrated "Doctor of the Voice"

Barbara Ruth Klein

You could make anyone sing!

❦

ACKNOWLEDGMENTS

I would like to extend special thanks to . . .

GENE ANTHONY, internationally recognized photographer, who was only one of two photographers allowed to take photos at the funeral of Marilyn Monroe. For more photo information, please go to geneanthony@earthlink.net.

RENEE MICHAELS, Marvelocity, Inc., for her editorial and consultative support.

IRA SHORE, President and CEO, Fine Art Management Corporation, for his generous guidance in marketing and licensing decisions.

SAM STERN, who discovered the *Misfits* photos, taken by Doc Kaminski, his longtime friend, for choosing to let the world know about their existence in *Marilyn, Joe & Me*. For photo information, contact Sam's associate, Jack Bacon, at www.jackbacon.com, or phone 775-322-1901.

KENNETH SEGURA KNOLL, founder and Executive Producer of Southwest Communication Services, Inc., for his management and creative contributions to the project.

. . . And to my loyal friends who always care; you are all special to me. You are my family: Mary Jane Popp and her husband, Erick Sprunger; Vicque Walton Kimmel and her husband, Jake; Violet (Vi) Wesner and her husband, Leon; Sally (Selma) Burger and her son, Ronald; Brenda Napolillo and her husband, Stephen; Claudette Auchu; Edra MacDowell; Ilana Ireland; Betty Schoeph.

Contents

ABOUT THE AUTHORS

Photo by Dennis Chapman

JUNE DiMAGGIO is the daughter of Louise (Lee) and Tom DiMaggio, brother of baseball icon Joe DiMaggio. *Marilyn, Joe & Me* is the first book written by a member of the very private DiMaggio family.

Ms. DiMaggio, whose family owned the famous DiMaggio's Restaurant on Fisherman's Wharf in San Francisco, knew Marilyn Monroe for eleven years. A musical theater star herself, Ms. DiMaggio knows firsthand the struggles beneath the glamour of Hollywood in the 1950s.

She appeared in several films, including *Ten Thousand Bedrooms*, starring Dean Martin. Her television credits include "Dead Line," "Wyatt Earp," "San Francisco Story," "Hey Jeannie," and "Tales of California."

A veteran of eleven musicals with the famed Music Circus, Ms. DiMaggio was featured in *Look* magazine in the 1950s. Her last musical role was in *Wonderful Town*, with Carol Channing at the Greek Theater. Her career also included numerous television commercials and radio appearances. Ms. DiMaggio has also been a popular lecturer about extrasensory perception (ESP).

Most important, Ms. DiMaggio, now in her late seventies, spent time with Marilyn—the person—and here sets the record straight: that her intelligent, funny, and openhearted friend did not commit suicide.

She knows, because her mother heard the voice of Marilyn's killer the night the legend died.

MARY JANE POPP has hosted and produced both radio and television locally and nationally for more than thirty years. She earned a bachelor of science degree in opera/speech/theater and a master of arts degree in speech/theater from Indiana University. She has also studied toward a doctorate degree in telecommunications.

Photo by Dennis Chapman

Ms. Popp is well known for the fast-moving syndicated radio magazine show "Poppoff," which she produces and hosts on CRN Digital Talk Radio. She also writes for three publications and an on-line column, "The Poppoff Report," at www.lamasbeauty.com, where she shares her thoughts and expertise on celebrities, lifestyles, and other topics. From politics to health and from presidents to Hollywood stars, Ms. Popp has built a strong reputation as an energetic and fair interviewer who presents topics of interest to a wide audience.

A consummate communicator, Ms. Popp studied with the famed "Voice Coach to the Stars," Barbara Klein, as did June DiMaggio and Marilyn Monroe. She's tirelessly hosted fund-raising telethons and inspired many as a motivational speaker. Ms. Popp has appeared in numerous theater productions, four movies, and countless singing venues.

She has served as writer, producer, and talent for more than three hundred radio and television commercials, and produced and hosted five television shows in addition to both reporting and anchoring TV news at several stations.

Ms. Popp has served on the boards of the Arthritis Foundation, the March of Dimes, the United Way, the Red Cross and others.

She is listed in the *International Directory of World Leadership* and *Who's Who In Women* and has received more than four thousand awards from the U.S. Air Force, the Red Cross, the California Highway Patrol, and the U.S. Army among many others.

A trusted celebrity interviewer, Ms. Popp spent seven years getting to know and interviewing June DiMaggio, to relate her memories in *Marilyn, Joe & Me.*

INTRODUCTION

By Mary Jane Popp

DURING MY THIRTY-YEAR media career, I have interviewed thousands of people in television, radio, and print from celebrities and authors to politicians and everyone in between. Whether it was Bob Hope or the Reagans, the Carters or Mr. Blackwell, my main goal has always been to get to the truth behind the story.

I love what I do, and I am committed to always stay the course of accuracy. As a result of my standards, celebrities and those close to them confide in me, knowing that they can trust me with their private thoughts and feelings.

June DiMaggio and I met in 1980 when I was producing and hosting radio and television talk shows in Sacramento, California. In previous years, I had interviewed many authors who said that they knew everything there was to know about Marilyn Monroe. Around that time I had one so-called expert on my show who claimed to know that ageless icon, and I received a rude awakening when my guest related tales about Marilyn's life and loves that shocked my sensibilities then and continue to do so even today.

Did I believe what he told me then? Probably. What source did I have to prove the information wrong? None. Anyone who knew for sure was dead, and the dead don't tell.

Then came a call from a woman named June DiMaggio.

At first I thought her call was a hoax, too. I thought that she was putting me on, but June soon made it clear to me that the "expert" storyteller was just that. In other words, he was full of it, and I don't mean praise. Her language was a bit more graphic than that, and I got the message.

June is the niece of Joe DiMaggio, recognized as the greatest baseball player ever. Until their passing, June's father and mother, Tom and Louise DiMaggio, owned DiMaggio's Restaurant on San Francisco's Fisherman's Wharf. With the opportunity to finally hear the truth from a family member, my dream to write a book from an insider's point of view seemed closer to fruition, but it would be twenty years before that came to pass.

I was thrilled that June chose me to work with her. It's been a once-in-a-lifetime experience to share the stories of her Uncle Joe, Marilyn Monroe, the DiMaggio family, and many other actors she knew and worked with in her career in Hollywood and on the stage.

Finally the truth will come out, I kept telling myself. No DiMaggio has ever written a book about the family's relationship with Marilyn and other stars. To have information come from such a reliable source was an offer I couldn't turn down. As June told me, "Uncle Joe DiMaggio was a very quiet man, and never spoke badly of anyone. He didn't even talk with reporters, afraid they might misquote him or take it out of context. It amazes me how so much is written about Joe even though he never granted a personal interview. I want you to hear all about the *real* Joe DiMaggio, not the rumors and innuendoes of so many who never really knew Joe or even spoke with him."

As for the Marilyn Monroe story, I discovered that June knew this incredible woman before she and Joe were married and for years after they divorced until the day she died. The stories poured out and this book began to take shape.

I never doubted that June's words deserved to be written down. Through all the years of talking with her, I discovered the immensely rich life she's led. As a wonderful bonus, June and I have become close, like family. Through her reminiscences I now know what the monumental DiMaggio family—and all the exciting people who came into their lives, including June's friend, the great Marilyn Monroe—were really like.

"I guess Marilyn and I got along so well because we were so close in age," June said. "And with both of us being in show business, we had much in common."

Sadly, the world would never see the true potential of this wonderful person. While her death has been shrouded in conjecture and speculation, now you will hear the truth of Marilyn's tragic, final day. The glitter of Joe's and Marilyn's lives is well-documented in photographs and print. Now I am honored to help show you the very heart and soul of those who were a part of their story through the memories of a family member.

1

TWIN SISTERS-IN-LAW

THERE'S A MYSTIQUE surrounding any great icon, but as I, June DiMaggio, learned again and again, behind every one of them is a real person with honest feelings and authentic tragedies as well as triumphs.

I have known many a celebrity, and some quite well. I lived that life, too, and experienced many of those same hills and valleys. It's so much easier to see them when someone else is making a mistake than when you're making one of your own.

Does what you hear about you and your family ever sound like fiction, that people are talking about total strangers? At times, that's exactly how I feel, given the fanciful stories told about me and my family and friends.

There is a certain amount of interpretation in recounting a story, I realize, but these days it seems that the nastier the story, the better it sells. Too often these stories include exaggeration to the point that they become total garbage; the truth be damned. I believe in writing the truth and letting the cards fall where they may.

I feel outraged and deeply hurt when I read so many lies about my friend Marilyn Monroe, still adored throughout the world. Now, years after her death, writers who never spent time with her or never knew her as I did seem to be able to get away with all the lies and distortions they want. The facts may not be as spicy and as titillating as you have been conditioned to hear, but they are the truth.

I know.

I was there.

Marilyn's birthday and mine were just a few days apart. Hers was on June 1, 1926, and mine is June 11, 1928. We are both Geminis, and our astrological sign tells much about our characters. Like me, Marilyn was very emotional. We were both easily hurt and could sulk for a time, but Geminis have dual personalities, which helps us snap out of our funks very quickly, too.

With true Gemini vulnerability, Marilyn was sensitive and fragile, easily hurt. She and I could present one face and persona to the world while hiding our deep inner pain. To me, Norma Jeane Baker was simply a girl who wanted to be a dramatic actress. Marilyn, or Marilee as I called her, was a darling—a woman, yes, but also a lost little child. We spent time together sharing, dreaming, and exchanging our hearts' desires until the very day of her death. The stories I share with you are from my personal friendship with this great Hollywood legend.

After her divorce from Uncle Joe in 1954, I became very close to the real Marilyn, a confused and lonely young woman. How many women dream of being a star like she was, imagining the fame and fortune that most of us only read about? Only a very few would prefer to live like the ordinary folks they see next door, yet Marilee was one such woman. She was a little girl in many ways and not the resplendent, confident screen idol whose image haunted her until she left us much too soon. Her real goal was to live an ordinary life, doing ordinary things.

I believe that Marilyn would have been happy as a stay-at-home mom with children of her own and a family to care for. She needed to be needed, but that wasn't meant to be. She was meant to be a star, and fate took hold.

I don't think the vast amounts of money she made meant that much to her. I'm sure she enjoyed the financial rewards, but security in Hollywood is fleeting. She did, however, love being generous. I still have several presents that she gave to my mother Lee, my friend Barbara Klein, and me.

I don't want to portray her as someone who lived all her life in sadness. She had wonderful times, too, many with me. Marilyn and I could chat for hours on end about all sorts of things: from our respective careers in Hollywood to poets and literature to the loves in our lives. It was she who taught me that life can be beautiful with only the simple pleasures.

THANKS TO THE NAME DIMAGGIO, my parents' restaurant was famous in San Francisco and far beyond. Why? In part because of the famous name of my Uncle Joe, who was born on November 25, 1914. In 1933 he started out playing baseball with the Pacific Coast League's San Francisco Seals. He worked very hard and logged hours of play and concentration, developing his innate abilities for the Big Leagues. Joe's ultimate dream was to be the best, and to this day he's often called the best baseball player in the history of the game.

My family related story after story about how he spent hours on the baseball diamond perfecting his abilities, yet he never complained about his time there, no matter how grueling. He loved to play ball, pure and simple. I think it was built into his very being. He had natural, God-given talents, but he honed those instinctive abilities to reach heights that few sports idols ever do. Joe was considered one of the most gifted batters in professional baseball history.

In his quest to reach those heights, he also obtained the respect and adoration of the public. His extraordinary talent made him an American hero. To this day I have the watch that Uncle Joe gave my father. It was given to him in 1938 as a tribute from the San Francisco

 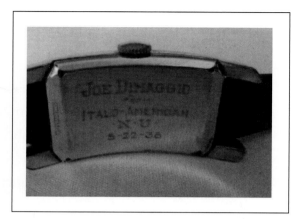

When my Uncle Joe became a New York Yankees player in 1938, the Italo-American N.U. in San Francisco gave him this watch. By the way, it still runs—they don't make 'em like they used to.

Italo-American organization for making it to the Big Leagues—the New York Yankees—after his stint with the Seals.

I also treasure the World Series ball from 1951, his best and last year in baseball, and the year Joe retired from the game. It bears the signatures of players who represent the best in sports history: Mickey Mantle, Yogi Berra, Billy Martin, along with the rest of the team and, naturally, Joe himself. When he played in that 1951 World Series, he earned about $100,000. Of course, Joe DiMaggio began in baseball for a lot less than that, earning about $25,000 a season because in those days athletes played for the love of the game, not for huge salaries, as they do today.

NOT TO BRAG, BUT MY FATHER, TOM, was considered the sports brain of the family, and early on he managed Joe's career to get him started on the right track. Very few people aside from Joe knew that my father

I treasure this baseball from the 1951 World Series—the last World Series my Uncle Joe played in.

was a wonderful baseball player in his own right. Even Joe admitted quite openly that my father was by far the better athlete. With his natural athletic skills, my father would have surpassed his other brothers' excellence on the baseball field.

Fate, however, denied him the chance to play in the Big Leagues. Early in his life he injured his back and shoulder in a freak accident, but as a DiMaggio, Father didn't sit and cry about it, and the damage didn't stop him from becoming a handball champion. During the 1940s he won trophy after trophy at the Dolphin Club in San Francisco. Although my father couldn't fulfill his own athletic dreams, he was devoted to managing his brother's career for quite some time.

Tom and Joe were close. They would talk for hours about profound issues such as the universe and the meaning of life. On clear evenings, the two brothers climbed to the roof of my parents' apartment building in San Francisco, gazing into the night sky for hours on end. Father had a library of books on astronomy, and Joe's curiosity was insatiable.

Tom had another innate ability: catching fresh fish. It was in his blood from his father's side of the family. My grandfather was a fisherman in Sicily. My Sicilian grandmother Rosalee was from Isola de Femme, where they met. His brothers—Joe, Mike, Vincent, and Dominic—all started out as fishermen, and Mike and Tom carried on the family tradition. It was a sizeable operation. Their nets spread out along an entire block at the docks on Fisherman's Wharf.

My father had never even considered opening a restaurant. He loved what he was good at, being a commercial fisherman. While he was still setting out to sea, my mother and Aunt Ruth Rovegno Roselli opened a hotel-restaurant and bar and called it Rovegno's.

They were just following yet another family tradition. Many years before, my grandfather on my mother's side ran a hugely successful restaurant in Pleasanton, California. His two girls grew up in this business atmosphere, so it was only natural that my mother and aunt opened a place of their own.

On Larkin Street, between California and Polk Streets in San Francisco, Rovegno's was an Italian haven with authentic dishes inspired by Aunt Ruth. As a child, I couldn't get all my "ths" in order and called her "Annie Rudie." Everyone else started calling her that as well, and she loved it.

Rovegno's was a popular San Francisco mainstay for many years, serving all kinds of wonderful foods with Italian flair. While my mother was a good cook, my Annie Rudie was an exquisite chef. She became renowned for her chicken cacciatore and homemade ravioli with special sauces from her father's recipes. She made all the raviolis by hand, adding a secret ingredient. And oh, they were delicious! What was the defining ingredient? She swore us to secrecy, and I know she would come back from the grave to haunt me if I told, but I can say it took a lot of brainpower, which should give you a big hint.

My cousin Gloria, our friend Anita, and I helped out in the hotel and restaurant, too. We made up the beds on Saturdays so that the maid could take the day off. It didn't matter that we were DiMaggios. We weren't coddled in those days. We had chores to do, and they had to get done and done right. Mother and Annie Rudie would pay the three of us with a movie matinee at the Polk Street Royal Theatre. Back then it cost a whopping ten cents to see a double feature. Mother always made sure we had enough for the movie plus an extra twenty-five cents to spend next door at the Red Poppy Candy Shop.

THE FAMILY TRADITION OF HOSTING celebrities—from powerful politicians to Hollywood stars—began at Rovegno's and continued at DiMaggio's Restaurant. Owing to Uncle Joe's prominence, the DiMaggio name made it hugely successful, but my mother was the business brain behind its reputation.

I can't remember ever *not* being in or around show business. The bug bit me when I was about nine years old, and I appeared in the play *Little Red Riding Hood* at a synagogue. And I'm a Mormon! My grandmother pretty much raised me, teaching me the tenets of the Mormon religion. Mother and Father were very busy with their work, so Grandmother took over the daily raising. There were no day-care centers back then, and family took care of family.

Although I will never forget my terror when I first stepped on-stage—to play the part of a perfect tree—theater was in my blood.

Here's me, "Little Baby June," on camera with my first acting partner.

Me again, "Little Junie" (the tree), launching my acting career at the synagogue.

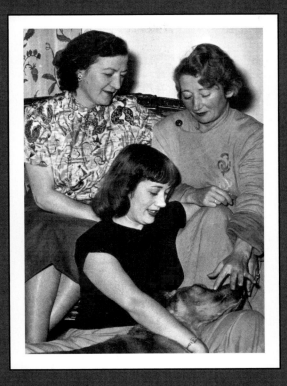

Left to right: Annie Rudie, Louise (Lee), and June. Annie Rudie was always there—she and my mother were very close. Pedy and I loved being with them.

My father, Tom, meeting my grandmother, Mama DiMaggio, at the San Francisco Airport after her return from New York. This was tradition the Italian way.

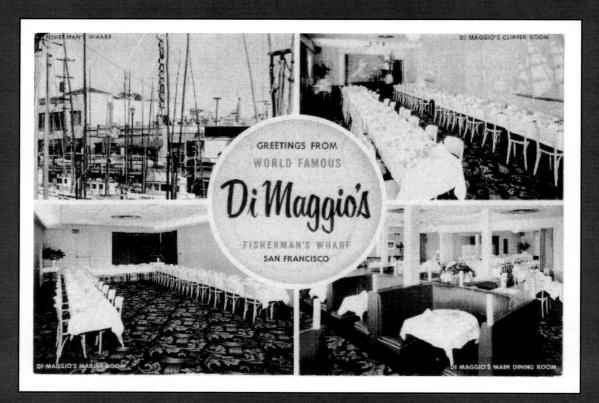

FISHERMAN'S WHARF

DI MAGGIO'S CLIPPER ROOM

GREETINGS FROM
WORLD FAMOUS
Di Maggio's
FISHERMAN'S WHARF
SAN FRANCISCO

DI MAGGIO'S MARINE ROOM

DI MAGGIO'S MAIN DINING ROOM

Known for its great cuisine and celebrities,
DiMaggio's Restaurant beat the opening of the
Golden Gate Bridge by one day.

You can take the man
out of the fishing boat,
but you can't take the
fisherman out of the
man. Fishing was
bred into my
father, Tom DiMaggio,
who started as a
commercial fisherman
and remained one
until the day he died.

Dad, Mom, and me in a quiet moment.

*My father, Tom, and his childhood friend,
Reno Barsocchini, show off the DiMaggio baseball
legacy at DiMaggio's Restaurant.*

When I turned nine, my parents felt it was time for me to enter contests. While I would eventually perform onstage as a singer-actress, I began my career playing the piano. My mother had me take lessons from the unforgettable ol' Mrs. Stohl, a Mormon, who was quite the disciplinarian.

Her starched look and manner remain in my memory like a scrapbook photo. She charged all of $2.00 a lesson, a pretty stiff rate back in the 1930s. I studied with her for about a year and won several prizes, but honestly, I was scared to death. I can still hear the strains of the piece I was playing at a concert, Gershwin's "Rhapsody in Blue." I sat at the piano, my hands shaking. Strange that I was so frightened at the piano, but never when I sang.

And I did win the contest, although to this day I don't know how, unless the others were much worse than I was.

ANNIE RUDIE WAS THE NURTURER in our family, but when it came to business, my mother ruled with an iron fist. She was a financial whiz and not afraid to throw her weight around, even if she was a tiny 5'1", weighing barely 100 pounds. She had the foresight to envision the potential growth in San Francisco and, boy, was she right. It was she who convinced my father to give up his commercial fishing business and buy the Fisherman's Wharf property.

After my mother and aunt sold Rovegno's, Mother bought land on Jefferson Street to open the first DiMaggio's Restaurant, a small, first-floor seafood stop. Uncle Joe also invested in the restaurant, so when it opened it was called Joe DiMaggio's Seafood Grotto. We beat the opening of the Golden Gate Bridge by one day.

Joe DiMaggio had played baseball for the Seals for quite a few years by this time, and in San Francisco his name carried a lot of weight, especially after he moved on to play with the New York Yankees.

As the restaurant's popularity grew, my parents added a second story and moved the restaurant upstairs. It became a first-class dining establishment serving steaks, chops, fabulous fresh fish, and incredible Italian delicacies. The name became shortened to DiMaggio's, and soon it became a landmark.

So Father went from being a world-class commercial fisherman to one of San Francisco's best-known and respected restaurateurs. He was written up in many trade magazines for his top-quality fish and the best steaks in town.

The food, the atmosphere, and of course the DiMaggio name drew famous clientele, but my father believed in serving hearty portions at reasonable prices to all comers, not just the rich and famous. Father always reminded me of singer Perry Como. It was not unusual for him to break into song with a Neapolitan tribute or two. In truth, he was a pretty good singer, quite unlike his brothers Joe and Vince, who couldn't carry a tune in a bucket.

My father still loved the ocean and personally caught much of the fish served at DiMaggio's. Uncle Joe gave my father the *Yankee Clipper*, the Chris Craft boat presented to him at Yankee Stadium in 1949 on Joe DiMaggio Day. He said he had no personal use for it, so why not turn it into a fishing boat? I suspect that Joe had an ulterior motive. He and my dad loved to go out fishing together, which they did regularly. Father never broke his Wednesday routine of taking the boat out until six months before his death, when he just couldn't handle skippering anymore.

Father was soft-spoken, never boisterous, and of strong character. Always a gentle man, he never raised his voice or lost his temper.

One stormy day at sea, he jumped off his boat to save a drowning man, with no consideration for his own safety. The story was recounted over and over at family gatherings, but Father would just listen modestly and quickly change the subject.

So many times he gave of himself with no thought to the consequences, like the time he rescued a woman from an apartment fire that started from a lit cigarette. He broke down the door and carried her to safety. With no concern for commendations or notoriety, he simply saw it as a job that needed to be done.

To the end of his life, my father never spoke of his heroism. That wasn't his way. He was from the old school that placed honor above all else. One might say that's a trait he shared with his famous brother.

2

MEETING JEANETTE AND MORTIFIED IN CHINATOWN

MOTHER AND GRANDMOTHER KNEW how much I loved the movies and always let me go to Saturday matinees. When I was eleven, one of the first movies I saw was *Naughty Marietta,* starring Jeanette MacDonald. From that moment, I wanted to become a singer just like that glorious lady. I went to every new picture of hers as well as to her older ones, never tiring of her wondrous voice and the warmth she projected.

Then I heard that Jeanette MacDonald's concert tour was coming to San Francisco. I was just a child, mind you, but using my determination, I managed to get to the theater on my own. I diligently stood at the stage entrance, hoping against hope that I would catch a glimpse of the woman who had kindled my passion for singing.

A huge car drove up and, as Jeanette MacDonald exited the car and stood to her full height—a feisty 5'4" tall—it was all I could do to keep myself from jumping in front of her. Instinctively I reached for her arm. To my amazement, she reached out and let me, a little Italian girl, escort her arm in arm to the stage door.

I walked alongside this wonderful woman, my heart pounding in my chest, but sinking as well. It was my dream to see the great Jeanette MacDonald perform live, but as we neared the stage door, I became more and more tentative. This tender woman could sense something was wrong and asked me what it was.

I was heartbroken. I told her that I didn't have enough money to buy a ticket to see her perform that night. Well, she marched me right into the theater and let me watch her entire performance from the wings. I was on cloud nine. The thrill of my young life had come true because of this wonderful actress who shared so much with so many. Jeanette could never have imagined how her single act of generosity impacted my life. After that chance encounter, I walked on air for weeks.

To this day I credit Jeanette MacDonald's influence for my enthusiasm in my profession. Time passes so quickly, and it would be many years before I would get to see her again. Tragically, it was very near the end of her life, which ended way too early.

BACK IN THE EARLY '40s when I was a teenager, our family would gather at my parents' home, and I will never forget how Uncle Joe would greet each of us with a big hug and kiss. He was a muscular guy and, when he hugged me, it literally took my breath away. I don't care how many stories exist about his being cold and unemotional, the warmth Joe felt for his family never diminished. That was the Italian in Joe.

Thanksgiving and Christmas were always special times when we all, Joe included, would gather at DiMaggio's to feast and give thanks. There was laughter and song and food to satisfy any appetite. Joe cherished his private time, and he never brought any guests, including his first wife, Dorothy Arnold, until he met Marilyn.

After he and Dorothy divorced, Joe could have had any woman to accompany him, but he wanted to be with just family. He valued his privacy above all else until the day he died. That's why he never granted interviews about his personal life and why so much of what you hear is mere speculation. The next time you hear stories of his being abusive to Marilyn and aloof to those close to him, remember how those bear hugs took my breath away and how much Joe valued his family.

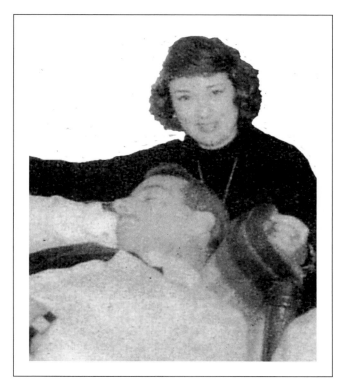

Uncle Joe was just a laid-back kind of guy when he wasn't in the public eye. I got such a kick out of him sacking out on my lap.

The great Joe DiMaggio, utterly aware of his public image, was never seen with a cigarette in his mouth in any publicity picture, at any game or personal appearance, or at any public place where kids were present. The truth, however, is that yes, he did smoke, and yes, he had a drink once in a while.

In fact, he loved his cigarettes, as did my mother. I remember her once saying that if she liked cigarettes any better, she would eat the butts. Joe would always say "ditto" to that, but he felt strongly that he had to keep his public persona pristine for the young people who saw him as a role model.

Many times I saw him enjoying bull sessions with friends in the bar at DiMaggio's, but when a family with children came in, he extinguished his cigarette, set down his drink, and went into the dining area.

It was rare to see my Uncle Joe with a cigarette, and you never would when children were around.

He never wanted his young fans to see him doing anything that would tarnish their image of Joltin' Joe. You would have never seen Joe linked with drugs in the headlines.

Due to his fame, Joe knew many headliners, including Frank Sinatra, but Joe also had strong feelings about maintaining a good reputation. When he heard a whisper that Frank might have been involved with the Mafia, it was enough to make him distance himself from "The Boss." Joe had a total disdain for anything that had to do with the Mafia.

Of course, many celebrities came through the doors of DiMaggio's simply because of Joe. For the forty-six years it was open, DiMaggio's became a Mecca for celebrities, including Sophie Tucker, Hoagy Carmichael, golf legend Arnold Palmer and, of course, top baseball players from Mickey Mantle to Ted Williams. Even the famous madam Sally Stanford, who later became mayor of Sausalito, was welcome there.

Joe brought many of his celebrity friends to dine, and often to conduct business. Lots of million-dollar contracts were discussed over good cooking in the private back room, but one thing was for sure: at

DiMaggio's everyone was treated the same no matter who they were, star or not. Long before it was in vogue, my father saw to it that DiMaggio's was an equal-opportunity dining establishment.

I remember vividly when Joe Louis, the heavyweight boxing champion of the world, was in town. Uncle Joe was a big fan of his, but those were very different times. African Americans were unwelcome in most white-owned restaurants, and prejudice abounded. Louis, knowing this, offered that the pair go through the tradesmen's entrance.

Both Joe and my father were terribly upset and insisted the champ enter the main door like everyone else, but Louis, great man that he was, realized that his presence could encourage others of color to follow. If that happened, he knew that DiMaggio's would likely come under protest, which could devastate the business.

My mother and father were very close, but even he couldn't separate mother from her cigarettes.

In the end, Joe DiMaggio and Joe Louis enjoyed a cozy dinner together in the kitchen. I can still hear the respect in my father's voice for this caring man. For many years after that incident, Father would say, "Joe Louis is not only a great fighter, but a great man."

SINCE I WAS CULTIVATING my love of singing, Mother decided it would be a good idea for me to join my junior high school choral group. The choral teacher had discovered I had a good voice, but it was too big for the chorus. The teacher called my mother and suggested that I take private lessons to become a soloist.

That's when my career began to take shape. Two voice teachers tried to make me into a coloratura, but a high-pitched coloratura I was not. My mother recognized this, and kept looking for someone who could bring out the best in me.

With some lessons behind me, I began to make the rounds at various functions, including the Italian Radio Hour at San Francisco's Fugazi Hall. Every good little Italian girl wanted to sing on the Italian Hour, and I performed on radio when I was just thirteen.

Those were the days when you sang wherever possible, whenever possible. I sang "Let's Sing Again," made famous by boy singer Bobby Breen. I won first prize: a week's performance at the Golden Gate Theatre, at a whopping $25.00 for the entire week. This was my very first professional job. Talk about a teen thrill!

Along with being on stage, I also enjoyed tennis as both a spectator and player, but I was too busy singing and acting to take an interest in other sports. When Uncle Joe invited me to go to my very first football game with him, I felt honored that he wanted to introduce me to the game. I was looking forward to our time to visit together, since I mostly saw him only at family gatherings.

The day of that Shriners' game must have been the coldest day of the century in the Bay Area. I bundled up, but wasn't really prepared for the wind that whipped in from the Pacific or the torrent of rain that drenched us to the bone. It was miserable weather. Rain poured down on us as we sat shivering under a big, black umbrella. It rained so hard that I couldn't see much of the action on the field. The players were way down at the other end, and I didn't know why, nor did I much care.

Bored to tears, cold and wet, I took it for as long as I possibly could, trying to please Joe for his heartfelt effort and to show interest as he explained what was going on in the game. When I couldn't take it any longer, I turned and looked up at him.

"I'm sorry, Joe," I started, thinking I could make up some excuse. Then I remembered how Joe believed in honesty. "I've had it. Can we please go home?"

I never told him the truth—that I'd hated every minute of the day—but in my way, with a big smile on my face, I added, "But I love baseball, Uncle Joe."

I could always make him smile with my cute, coy, little-girl act.

"I love baseball too, and we can leave if you want," he said with a laugh. As you've guessed, that was the first and last football game I ever attended.

Joe loved all kinds of sports and went to as many as he could. Another game he adored was golf. Until the day he died, at age eighty-four, he played golf with famous golfers such as Arnold Palmer and Jack Nicklaus. He retired to Florida and spent his last days on the golf course.

Another uncle, Vincent Paul DiMaggio, also played baseball from 1937 to 1946 in Boston, Cincinnati, Philadelphia, Pittsburgh, and even for a short stint in New York with the Giants. I think, however, that he used baseball as a springboard for his first love, singing. He wanted to be a stage idol like Frank Sinatra and other crooners of that era.

All successful, the brothers DiMaggio gather.
They all shared the middle name "Paul"
because their father revered St. Paul. Left to
right: Tom Paul, Vincent Paul, Joseph
Paul, and Dominic Paul.

Perhaps Mama
DiMaggio was
congratulating
Uncle Joe (a
Yankee), as his
brother Dom (a
Boston Red Sox
player) and
Uncle Joe's son
(Joe, Jr.) looked
on.

My father, Tom, and Uncle Joe enjoyed many sports together; bowling was one of them.

He worked hard preparing for his debut on one of the national variety shows of the time. Quite obviously, his last name got him the slot. Of course, they all expected him to be good.

 My mother, my father, Uncle Joe, and I all gathered around the TV set in my parents' apartment, which happened to be just around the corner from Joe's. I was just getting started in my own career, so I was all ears, ready to take notes. Finally, the host announced Vince's appearance. We had never heard him sing professionally, so we didn't know what to expect. You could have heard a pin drop; quite unusual whenever you had more than two DiMaggios in the same room.

Vince strutted onto the stage, smiling from ear to ear. The music began. He took a deep breath, and so did we. We held our breath, actually. None of us uttered a word throughout his entire song, but our eyebrows raised a good inch. Vince's vibrato wobbled so much that a truck could have driven through it. There was no expression in his song, and certainly no charisma.

Joe looked at my father, Father looked over at Mother, who finally looked wide-eyed at me. Finally, Tom turned to his brother Joe and said, "Pathetic!" None of us argued. That one word said it all.

Undeterred, Vince didn't give up immediately, but he lasted only one season singing on the club circuit, and that most likely because of our last name. I guess I was blessed to be the one professional singer in the family.

❧

WHEN I WAS ALMOST SWEET SIXTEEN, Jack MacBade stole my heart. I'll never forget the date when Jack took me to Chinatown for what we thought was a variety show at a theater. A buddy had given him the tickets, but didn't bother to tell him it was a burlesque show. When the bumping and grinding started, I shrank in my seat. The spectacle didn't let out until 11 P.M., which was too late to catch the last cable car home.

"Juniper," Jack said, using the pet name he called me, "I don't have cab fare."

It was midnight before we made it to my house on foot, and I knew it might as well have been 4:00 in the morning. Our family and Annie Rudie lived in the same building as Rovegno's, the hotel-restaurant Mother owned with her, and Annie Rudie met us at the door. Jackie took off like a scared rabbit, leaving me to face the music alone, but she didn't say a word.

I didn't get much sleep that night, dreading what was going to happen. I was surprised when Jack and his older brother Edward arrived in the morning, ostensibly to face my formidable mother before she lowered the boom. TNT comes in little packages and so did Mother.

Trying his best to smooth things out, Edward quickly explained that Jack had gotten tickets from his buddies, not knowing that they were for a burlesque show. Expecting the worst, he talked fast and furiously, hoping that his being there would help his forlorn brother.

"He's a good boy," Edward sputtered. Here was this six-foot young man staring down at this silent little woman, my mother, not knowing what else to say.

It seemed like forever before Mother pronounced her verdict. She looked Jackie squarely in the eye. *Here it comes*, I thought.

"For God's sake," she asked, "Did you at least learn anything?"

Before he could answer, Mother glanced my way.

"I couldn't look," I said. "I was too embarrassed."

It seems she'd made up her mind that if we told the truth, there would be no punishment. She said that if we had lied, she'd never have let us see each other again.

"Now, go have a good meal," she insisted. By then, the restaurant was open for breakfast.

Jackie truly cared for me, but since my future career was all I thought about, nothing serious ever materialized for us. I saw him again a few years later when I was doing a play in Los Angeles and Jack had joined the Coast Guard. "Juniper," he said, "I'm still in love with you. Will you marry me?"

I couldn't. I had moved on, but I'd learned a valuable lesson about telling the truth, no matter how horrible it seems at the time. Now, after all these years, that's just what I'm doing—about Marilyn, Joe, me, and other celebrities whose lives were overshadowed by their spectacular stardom.

ACTRESS MERLE OBERON had enjoyed hearing me sing and wanted me to perform at one of the fabulous bashes she was holding for some studio bigwig. Her home was in the San Fernando Valley, where in 1945 at the tender age of seventeen I first met swashbuckler and movie legend Errol Flynn. He didn't mince words; he told me he wanted me to go upstairs with him.

Naturally, everybody knew what it meant to go upstairs with this good-time guy, but I had heard all the rumors, so I was ready with an honest answer.

"I don't need a job and I don't need a man, but thanks for the offer anyway," I said. This was one star who wasn't used to being turned down, and I think it really threw him for a loop.

I had never played the casting couch game, and I wasn't about to start that night. I picked and chose who would be my lovers, and it was never to get a part, but because I wanted to make love—*real* love, not sex for work. I have to admit that Errol wasn't pushy; he simply shrugged and went off on the prowl. Plenty of other hopeful little starlets were ready to step up to the plate, or the bed, at a moment's notice.

That's the way it was, and that night I had my first inkling that this might not be the life I wanted after all.

3

THE SUICIDE SQUAD

In 1945 I ENTERED THE WORLD of show business by joining the Reginald Travers Shakespeare Company in San Francisco. The first production I appeared in was showing at the Geary Theater in San Francisco, and I played a saucy little French maid in *The Drunkard's Bride* with Raymond Burr, later of "Perry Mason" fame. You can imagine what it meant to a mere teenager to be working with a man that I could tell, even then, was destined for greatness. They even added a song for me, "Cupid Shot Me Down for You." And I got rave reviews. Reginald Travers and Burr were the best of friends, with the kind of close relationship that wasn't acceptable in those days. They had to remain private and closeted, or their careers would have come crashing down. With Travers and company I appeared in many Gilbert and Sullivan operettas as well as plays, and the characters I portrayed and interacted with became my friends for life.

At the time I was taking lessons from the Berlin Opera Company's Otto Shulman, the best voice teacher in the Bay Area. As his first student in this country, I even stood for him as witness when he became a U.S. citizen. But had it not been for one more very special happening, I doubt I'd have reached my full potential.

One of Otto's students was a woman named Barbara Klein, who was studying to become a voice teacher herself. Otto felt that the two of us would make a fine match. He had no idea how right he was, but I wouldn't know that until the war was over.

27

❦

ALTHOUGH I WAS YOUNG, I knew only too well what was happening overseas, and I wanted to entertain our troops. To go overseas alone, you had to be twenty-one. At the time, I had no one to accompany me. So I had to lie about my age with the help of those who shall remain nameless.

With a little elbow twisting, I got a dear boyfriend to put together the proper papers, claimed that I was of age and, presto, I was on my way. (That stunt plagued me a number of years later. For example, how do you explain to Social Security that you aren't really old enough to deserve their retirement checks?)

During the closing months of World War II, I made plenty of appearances with the USO, from Guam to the Marianas. We were called the Suicide Squad because the Pacific Theater was extremely dangerous. I was in good company, though, with the likes of Ray Milland, Frances Langford, and Carol Landis. We toured the camps and got as close to the front lines as we were allowed. We never even knew where we were going, other than troops would be there when we arrived. We had to perform in some unstable conditions. There were times when bullets flew. Those tours brought me so many unbelievable stories—funny, sad, and sentimental—that I'll remember all my life.

This next story helps explain why we entertainers were called the Suicide Squad. We were asked if we'd take a chance and go down to the front lines to entertain the boys who were dug in for the duration. One gal who played the concertina volunteered enthusiastically. In my naiveté, I piped up, too. "Sure, let's go." Little did I know what I was getting myself into.

So there we were, being shuttled across battlegrounds—bumping, and I do mean bumping—along in a military Jeep, concertina blaring and me singing every song I could think of as loudly as I could. Mud

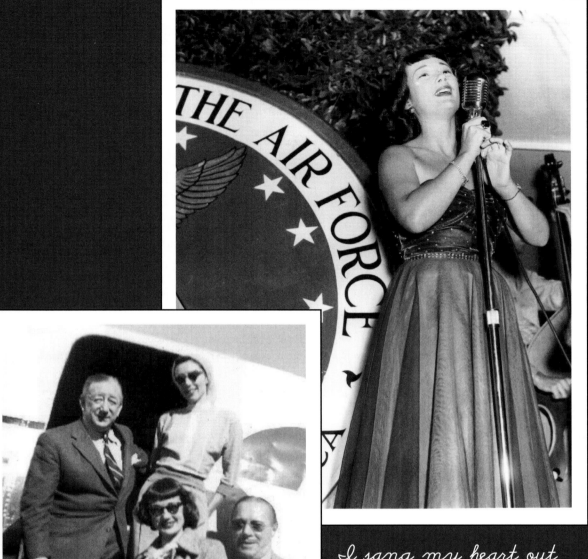

I sang my heart out for our boys wherever and whenever they wanted me to perform. It was the least I could do. (By the way, this is the dress I turned inside out and wore on stage.)

Oh, how I remember the plane rides as we flew into harm's way. We were called the "Suicide Squad" for good reason, but I wouldn't trade those days for a million bucks.

splashed our faces, but no amount of dirt was going to deter us from our mission. As I mentioned, we were young and dumb.

What happened next I can hardly believe, and I was there. We actually passed Japanese soldiers. They were just children themselves and, no, they did not fire at us; they waved to us with smiles as they listened to our music. We saw pain in their eyes, too. War is not pretty for either side, and no one wins, especially not those who have to fight. Keep in mind that we were just teenagers as well, not much older than these child-soldiers.

While we were there, not a shot was fired, thank God. We got to the front line, jumped out of the Jeep, and into the trenches we went, all set to cheer up our boys. Little did I know what was in store for me as we trudged along in those dirty, dismal mud pits, trying to keep up cheerful faces as we sang and smiled, smiled and sang—until I came upon one young soldier.

He couldn't have been much older than I was, and there he lay, all bloodied. His gunshot wounds were obviously severe and, even though I had no medical training, I could tell that he was dying. It was all I could do to keep my composure. Here, through the agony of this young man, the reality of war was staring me in the face.

I knelt by his side and cradled him in my arms. In such a soft voice, he told me his name was Mikey and asked if I would sing "When Irish Eyes Are Smiling." That song was very special to him because his mother always sang it when he was little. Looking into his eyes, I couldn't help feeling he'd become that little boy again. I almost couldn't sing for the lump in my throat, but for this brave young man who was dying for his country, for all of us, I told him I'd love to.

Then he asked me the hardest question of my life: Was he going to die? All I could tell him was that I didn't know, but everyone would do all they could to save him. I knew better, but I had to give him some peace of mind.

MARILYN, JOE & ME

A sense of serenity seemed to come over him, and he asked if I would do one more thing. Mikey asked me to tell his mother that he loved her. Of course I promised him I would, not knowing if I'd ever be able to fulfill his wish. I didn't know what else to tell him, so I quickly started singing, hoping it would help me get through. I'll never forget how he began breathing more and more slowly. Without my even knowing it until after I finished the song, he died. Despite the insanity around us, he passed away peacefully, quietly, in my arms.

That incident changed my life profoundly. I realized then that life is so fragile, and that I wanted to hold onto every moment as if it were my last. I won't ever forget the times I gave comfort to those who never returned to the wonderful life I was to enjoy.

Perhaps part of my youth and innocence died there with him. Part of me was left on the battleground in those godforsaken lands that ran red with the blood of our young men. But every minute I spent there in those barren fields, including the dangerous times, was worth it. Those servicemen gave me back so much more than they could have known.

Isn't it amazing how some things stay with you all your life? They don't have to be times with stars or in major roles on the stage and the big screen. Those war times were when I could make a difference that really counted, even if it was just one life at a time.

But then perhaps, that's what life is all about.

It was around Halloween 1945 when Barbara Klein and I met at Otto Shulman's. I was privileged to have met her at the start of her career, long before she achieved recognition as the famed "Vocal Coach to the Stars." Barbara had recently divorced her husband, an FBI agent named Polkinhorn, who was basically married to the Bureau—a career that didn't mix with Barbara's love of music and the gift she had for molding future singers. Strangely enough, she herself couldn't sing a single

The heart and soul of my performances came from my dear friend Barbara Klein, "Voice Coach to the Stars."

note, but she was a tremendous teacher. As a well-respected vocal teacher, she studied the physiology of the human voice to get to the core of each individual's potential. She could repair broken voices and make them soar, including those of a few singers still in the business today. Barbara's tutelage transformed me into a confident performer who never missed a beat on stage, and our wonderful relationship was to span some fifty-three years. But I'm getting ahead of myself.

Little did I know that Barbara had played an extraordinary role in the war. She was in Honolulu at the time of the attack on Pearl Harbor and exhibited great selflessness and courage by using her own vehicle to transport fallen soldiers from the USS *Arizona* to haven in Honolulu. Undaunted, she returned again and again, also driving a Red Cross truck, to bring wounded to the hospitals with no fear for her own safety.

President Franklin D. Roosevelt presented her with a citation for her bravery. Caring about people was always at the forefront of her life.

When World War II was over, I went on with my life, as we all did, putting those horrible moments behind me, or so I thought, until I was asked to sing for a parent-teacher association event in San Francisco. As always, Barbara came along to accompany me on the piano.

The crowd enjoyed my first couple of songs and some of the wartime stories about touring overseas that I shared. Then a woman raised her hand and, in a pleading voice, asked, "Did you actually sing for our boys?"

"Yes," I answered. Of all the many other stories I could have told, I'll never know why the incident of Mikey popped into my head, but it did. As I related the story that so changed my outlook on life, a hush came over the audience.

By the end of the story, I was in tears, and so was half the audience. The same lady who had asked me if I sang to the boys stood up. I was stunned to see that she was crying, and everyone could see her pain. Through her tears, she literally screamed out, "That was *my* Mikey!"

I could not believe this was happening. I didn't know what to say, so I finished my performance without another word about him.

Then the woman was instantly beside me, asking rapid-fire questions that I struggled to answer. I told her what information I could about her dying son, such as how at the end he passed on with no pain. Most important, I told her he wanted her to know that he loved her very much and that his final thoughts were of his mother.

She told us that Mikey was her only son, and she begged us to have dinner with her that evening. The military had told her that he died, but she'd never known where or how. How grateful she was to receive the truth about son's final moments.

I never saw her again, but for the rest of my life I will never forget the peace I gave her. She made it all worth it—Suicide Squad and all. Part of my soul will always remain on that battleground.

I CONTINUED TO PERFORM for servicemen, and more incredible incidents ensued. One time the pianist didn't show up at a Christmas show on a southern California military base. As if that wasn't bad enough, he was also supposed to play for the ballet and act as master of ceremonies, too.

I guess word had gotten around that I was a decent speaker, because in marched the director asking me to emcee. I was happy to do it, of course, but I had no idea what all the company names were and I had no time to check correct pronunciations. So I made up half the names and slurred over the rest. Who would know? Then they asked Barbara Klein, who accompanied me on the trip and on the piano, if she would play the score for the ballet. She had no time to even look it over. That's the only time I remember Barbara ever being petrified, but she and I managed to pull it off together.

The audience loved every minute of the program. It was a good lesson for me, too, because I learned that the audience never knows what you don't know unless you tell them. And you can bet we didn't! The boys loved not only the performance but the enthusiastic spirit we shared with them. That was one raucous night.

The whole atmosphere changed, however, as we were winding up the show singing Christmas carols. A hush fell over the audience that I had never witnessed before. Suddenly I realized that we on stage had become the families the servicemen had left behind. I can still see those young brave faces, and I vividly remember the tears we shared as their thoughts turned from the warmth and joy of that moment to shipping overseas to parts unknown. Who knew if they would ever return. At least we got to show them we cared for them. It is a moment that still lives in my heart.

Just three gals, hangin' out. That's Barbara with the beautiful smile on the left as my mother gives me a hug-and-a-half.

Another time we blew into a camp with no time to prepare anything, including our wardrobe changes. I realized that the dancer before me had on the same pink dress that I was going to wear for my performance. Well, I couldn't go on stage in the same exact dress, could I? So, thinking fast, I whipped off my dress just offstage and turned it inside out. The lining was a lovely silky gray. I had to be pinned in since the zipper was now showing, but I marched out onto that stage like a peacock, and no one in the audience was the wiser. To them this was an entirely different dress. I sang in top form, and I think it made my performance even better. Besides, all those guys wanted was to be entertained, and I was going to give them all I had.

Then there was the show in the States for the Army Air Corps, with me in a featured role. However, our leading lady didn't show up. It was a balmy night, and we were all exhausted from our trip to the camp, but the show had to go on, of course. Some five thousand homesick boys sat waiting, screaming, and stomping their feet in anticipation of terrific entertainment.

The director postponed as long as he dared, until he finally accepted that his leading lady was not coming. So he asked me to read her part—*and* mine! I said, "Sure," and he explained to the assembled servicemen that our star was delayed. Did they care? Not a hoot! They just wanted a show.

So there I was, playing the lead and my role as well. This was a first for me. I told the boys they would know when I was playing Elena because I would put on my glamour-girl sunglasses and, when I removed them, I would assume my other role. It was a real switcheroo for me, but the boys seemed to love the spectacle and really got into it. We could hear gunfire in the distance, probably on the firing ranges, but for that moment in time it was eons away. Halfway through the show, I got so tired of trying to keep up the charade that I just tossed the script into the audience. "Forget the script," I told them. "I'm here for you guys!" and I sang my heart out.

The guys went wild. At the end of my performance, and several standing ovations later, four soldiers hoisted me to their shoulders. We led the parade and the singing continued as they carried me back into camp. They thought that I had been such a trouper, not allowing a little thing like no lead actress to interrupt the performance. They made me feel like a real star! How could I not do my best for those wonderful young men?

Those are among the best times of my life. I vividly remember their faces and how much my performing meant to them. I'm sure many of them never returned home, but perhaps I gave them a brief respite during those tormented times.

4

ONE LOST LOVE, ONE ENDURING FRIEND

I CAN'T TELL YOU HOW NAÏVE I was back then. I was a child in this crazy business, but Barbara Klein kept me grounded. Without her I believe I might have been lost, like so many other show-biz souls. Ours was a relationship of women who loved each other as friends, not lovers. We did everything together, yet I had my own personal life and we both had many wonderful men in our lives.

I met Michael Van Zandt in 1945 at my mother's hotel-bar when I was around seventeen, but we didn't start dating immediately. It was later, after the war ended, that our lives intertwined. He was a pilot in the Army Air Corps. Having flown twenty-seven missions during the war, Michael was a real-life war hero, and I have to say that he was one sexy man, too. I was so in love with Michael that when he asked me to marry him, I said "yes" with no hesitation and all my heart.

His family—Manhattan socialites—had big bucks. So many times Mother told me, "It's just as easy to fall in love with a rich man as it is with a poor one." I kept that in mind, but I actually cared deeply for Michael. I was pleased to have fallen for a wonderful guy who just happened to be very well off. Michael and I planned to tie the knot and spend the rest of our lives together.

Barbara decided to throw us a huge engagement party. Michael's grandfather was so proud of his grandson's efforts on behalf of our country that he'd given him a plane. Michael was in New York until the morning of the party, when he planned to fly to Los Angeles to make the party in time that evening.

We all waited anxiously for Michael at the engagement party. This was to be the happiest moment in my life, but what was to be the beginning of our life together was not meant to happen. I never saw my Michael again. On the day our love was to be announced, his plane crashed and he was killed.

My heart was broken. My true love was gone forever. Some say true love comes but once in a lifetime. I, echoing another DiMaggio, would never love like that again. After my true love was gone, my only consolation was to throw myself into my work more than ever.

MY NEXT HURDLE CAME when my mother wouldn't let me go all by myself to southern California. I was almost twenty, but still a teenager after all. You can imagine what she was thinking. She wasn't sending her naïve young daughter to live among the big, bad wolves of Tinseltown. She wasn't about to let her little girl get in trouble. In truth, her fears were justified. Hollywood was a den of iniquity.

Barbara, nearly twelve years older than I was, came to my rescue by agreeing to move with me to Hollywood. We rented a place at 421 North Doheny Drive in Beverly Hills, and she opened a vocal studio across the street. We transformed what had been a quaint little florist's shop into the Barbara Klein Vocal Studio, and Barbara booked her first student in just three weeks.

Many stars regularly entered her vocal studio, and our home. Barbara was an inspiration to all her students, from greats like Jeanette MacDonald, Peggy Lee, and Marilyn Monroe to little-known talents who simply wanted her to help them sing better.

Barbie, as I called her, fixed many broken voices and made them

Barbara Klein's Vocal Studio was transformed from a floral shop into a celebrity stop.

whole again. She never tried to *change* anyone's voice. Instead she helped each voice to be the best it could be through exercises and a rebirth of each person's inner spirituality. Maybe her inability to sing a single note explains why she had no ego, just the desire to make others shine with their own glorious voices.

Barbara's teaching style was never off-the-rack or one-size-fits-all. She let each singer be who he or she innately was.

"Each person is unique," she said. "So how can you teach one style for every individual?"

Barbara always looked for the soul of the singer, whether the musical style was country, pop, or classical. She had a gift for recognizing star quality, too. Mary Jane, my co-author, has that kind of true charisma and a soul to match. Barbara told me many times that Mary Jane has star quality, an essence that doesn't come along very often.

As roommates and friends, Barbara and I never got in each other's way. I dearly loved to do housework and cook—I guess that's the Italian in me. Barbie always thanked me for all I did for her, but it was the least I could do for all she did for me; for the incredible influence she had on my life. In turn I had a positive effect on her life in many ways.

Barbie was very intelligent, but not an aggressive, high-energy woman. She had a reserved German personality and was rather laid back, perhaps traits she developed in order to deal with the volatile personalities she encountered in the entertainment industry. I think she acted reserved around the show-biz crowd out of her tremendous admiration for their work. To the end she was in awe of their achievements.

I taught her how to deal with stars, a skill I had ample opportunity to develop even as a child. To me celebrities were just people who had fallen—or risen—into extraordinary circumstances. For example, my Uncle Joe was a ballplayer to me, not a world-famous sports hero. I knew too well that celebrities faced the same likes and dislikes, the same loves and betrayals, the same ups and downs as we all do in life.

I helped Barbie understand that she was her star pupils' equal no matter how famous they were. Because a name appeared on a marquee meant only that the person behind that stardom counted. Eventually she came to accept them as I did, as just regular folks like everyone else who happened to have extraordinary skills.

Back then I was a hugger and a gusher who wore my emotions on my sleeve. I guess I still am, but giving a big hug was difficult for her in our early friendship. It was important for me to get Barbie to understand that emotion was an integral part of show biz, and she once told me how I opened a door in her thinking.

Like a caterpillar going through a metamorphosis, Barbie was a butterfly emerging from a cocoon, giving so much to stars and ordinary folk alike.

"What the caterpillar calls the end of the world, the Master calls a butterfly," she often said.

A month after her passing, my co-author Mary Jane brought me a huge butterfly balloon in Barbara's memory. You might not believe this, but that balloon, which Mary Jane brought me in 1998, is still filled with air, floating in my foyer.

I'll never forget when Barbie said to me one day, "Junie, I'm Italian now!" All of a sudden she felt that she could share warmth and show affection more freely. I felt privileged to have given back a little to this wonderful woman who did so much for me and so many others.

IF YOU'RE ITALIAN, food is not only sustenance, but the basis for social gatherings. Joe had a passion for two dishes in particular. One was chili, which I made whenever he came to southern California. Not your typical chili, this was a hearty mix that stuck to your ribs. Mother would take crumbled ground round or top sirloin, add Grandma's Chili Powder (which she loved because it wasn't hot, but had great taste). and then drop in some chopped yellow onion and salt. This wasn't soup. It was a substantial entree that went well with her other two side dishes: mashed kidney beans with a touch of butter, and rice with a sprinkling of Grandma's Chili Powder.

The other dish Uncle Joe (and later, Marilyn) really enjoyed was boiled beef. There was a trick to making something that sounds so simple into a very special dish. Mother used beef short ribs to create soup with a kick. To the short ribs she added yellow onions, pepper, salt, and a little chopped red pepper. When that had boiled until the beef was tender, she added ditalini, or little macaronis, for the finishing touch. It was another simple dish that was sensationally substantial.

Mother taught Dorothy Arnold, Joe's first wife, how to make the hearty chili and boiled beef, and later taught Marilyn as well. Each woman wanted to make her husband happy and believed (as practically everyone did back then) that the way to a man's heart is through his stomach. Being Italian, of course, Uncle Joe loved his lasagna, and when he came to visit my parents they always served it, along with the news of the neighborhood.

NEVER DID I HEAR Joe badmouth anyone for any reason. He knew that my grandmother had brought me up a Mormon, and one time he told me, "June, one of the greatest sins in the Mormon religion is hypocrisy. Never be a hypocrite."

I always followed that path. Although Joe was raised Catholic, he lived by that Mormon principle and believed that a true friend never says unkind things. Other sayings he was fond of were the old adages, such as "What goes around comes around," and "If you can't say something good about someone, say nothing at all," but the motto that Joe lived by was, "A man without integrity is a man without worth." Uncle Joe maintained his dignity and grace until the day he died.

When it came to family, he was always a no-nonsense business-man and used his influence to the max. In 1948, when I was starting out in show business, my agent wanted me to take some parts that I didn't feel were of a sufficiently high caliber. They were gun molls and prostitutes. He tried to make me believe that it was all good experience and that better parts would come along as a result, but something deep inside me knew better. I had seen too many stars get caught up in stereotypes, never to escape.

Later in life, when I met Marilyn Monroe, my feelings would be validated. Early in my career my agent didn't seem to care what role I took on, as long as he got his commission. That included not caring much if I were put on display because of my ample bosom.

Being young and inexperienced I didn't yet know how to handle the situation, so I turned to Uncle Joe for advice.

"Never let any agent take advantage of you," he warned me. "You want an agent who cares about you, not one who, if you get run over by a taxi, wouldn't care and will just sign up someone else."

That advice stayed with me for my entire career. Years later, when I ran into another problem with an agent, memory of that situation, which I had conquered successfully with Joe's help, came back to bolster me.

IN 1949, AS I NEARED the magical age of twenty-one, I had a total awakening. Through Olive Marlow, a friend of Barbara's, I met the great actress Eugenie Leontovich. Olive, also a singer, was married to Raymond Marlow, the famous tenor who played the Schubert Theatre circuit. Because of that meeting (and my talent), I became a featured player at Eugenie Leontovich's Stage Theatre in Beverly Hills.

Russian born, Eugenie was very well known for her work on Broadway. Being an actress-singer got me many more roles, because singing parts alone were not that plentiful. At the Holloway School of Theatre in the early 1940s, I studied only voice and diction, not acting, but I found that I had a natural knack for acting.

That was where I met Carol Channing. We both worked our way through the school by typing and walking Holloway's dog, Sergeant, and we shared our hopes and dreams. Those may have been lean years, but that's where friendships began and endured. I was raring to meet the world, and Carol was my friend and protector.

At such a young age, I found it amazing to be part of this special company of extraordinary talent. Eugenie would ask, "When is a theater not a theater?" and then fire back, "When it is a building. A theater needs no building!" Even though this Russian-American actress was a Broadway star of great note, she wanted to direct, but this was the late '40s, and women just did not cross certain lines. A woman could perform, but could she be in charge of the production? No.

Still, Eugenie circumvented the customs of the day and opened the Stage Theatre, where she not only starred in shows, but also directed them. I was fortunate that she recognized my talent early on, casting me in two delightful productions.

In 1949 she starred opposite Donald Porter in *And So to Bed.* I also had a part. With me in the play was a marvelous jazz guitarist, Earl Colbert. Earl had a wonderful bass voice and had always wanted to sing. After his time in the service, he began taking vocal coaching from Barbara Klein, paid for by the G.I. Bill. Earl and I did several shows together, but he got too serious about me. He wanted more of my precious time in those days than I could give to him, and so, no more jazz for June.

Also in 1949 Eugenie needed a vixen for *Dear Virtue* at the Stage Theatre. I was happy to oblige. What a thrill it was to be working with such great artists.

By the way, back then I was known as June Alpino. We made up the name by taking *Alp-* to represent my mother's Swiss-German background and *-ino* for my dad's Italian heritage. Today it sounds silly, but then I didn't want to be recognized just for being a DiMaggio. I wanted to be accepted on my own merits, not my name. I was thrilled when the extraordinary Leontovich told me that I was a good singer and a hell of an actress.

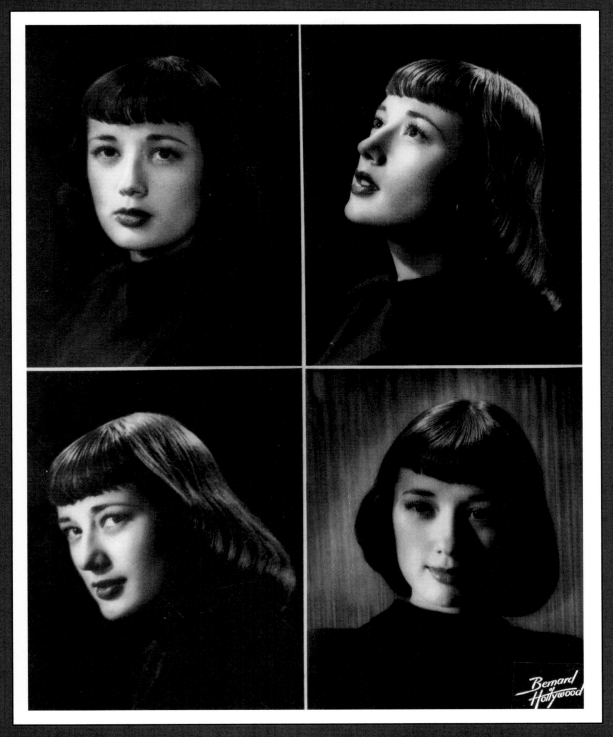

My many moods (head shots from Hollywood).

My head might have gotten way too big, so thank heavens I had Barbie to keep me on the straight and narrow. Her coaching gave me the tools I needed to be recognized at that time. Once I had established myself in the entertainment industry, I felt comfortable going back to my family name without feeling I was trading on the DiMaggio name.

5

PAYING THE PRICE OF CELEBRITY

AMID THE FRUSTRATIONS and instability of their hectic lives, many stars in Hollywood lost their way—some also lost their souls in the process—while others soared high. One of those lost souls was Kent Taylor, of "Boston Blackie" fame, who made quite a few films with Bette Davis and other up-and-coming starlets.

Kent had heard about Barbara's success as a voice teacher. Although known for his acting, he loved to sing in his very good baritone voice and wanted someone to help him develop as a performer.

Hollywood exploited stars' attributes for financial gain, never caring what they wanted out of life. Kent was the handsome leading-man type, and studio moguls didn't want him to sing, but he came to Barbara's studio for lessons anyway every single week.

He wanted so much to perform, but he had one major problem: He was terribly nervous when on stage by himself. More than butterflies in his stomach, he had a swarm of wasps that petrified him. That always seemed strange to me, as my nerves were never a bother. They weren't for Kent, either, when he was in front of the camera, but let him open his mouth to sing and stage fright became his undoing.

To soothe his nerves he asked if I would sing with him. Together we worked up a great act. He would solo with his favorite number, "I Believe." We would share duets like "Wanting You" from *New Moon* and "I Hear Singing and There's No One There." Then I'd solo with one of my signature songs, "One Night of Love." We added a little soft shoe and the act looked like a real winner.

Kent's talent agency thought our act was good enough for us to take on tour to promote his "Boston Blackie" series, but a dark shadow fell over our quest for success. At a Red Cross performance, with Kent's wife in the audience, the proverbial manure hit the ventilation system. If ever there was a face full of hate and contempt, it belonged to Kent's wife. I couldn't understand why she was looking daggers at me. Our performance was a success that night, but afterward she wouldn't speak to me. I remained totally in the dark as to why all the hate prevailed until the next day, when Kent came to Barbara's studio in tears. He explained that his wife was very jealous and absolutely refused to let him go on the road with me.

Before we got together, Kent was an alcoholic. When he got serious about singing, he dried out and focused on our tour. He knew I could help with his onstage nerves and, since I didn't drink, I could also help him stay dry. The only partying we ever did together was to visit the ice cream parlor for a soda.

I looked at Kent in utter surprise. "Is this woman your wife or your mother?" He explained that she held the purse strings and had total authority over his career—a revelation that came as a shock to Barbara and me. He and I had worked so hard. Now, because of her jealousy, was it all going down the drain?

Taking the initiative, Barbara called Kent's wife and explained that she had nothing to worry about. "If you still have misgivings, June's boyfriend could go along with them on the tour to set your mind at ease."

Her answer was still a big "No!" Kent was devastated. He desperately wanted to sing, which also would have boosted his somewhat sagging acting career. Then, a short time later, he lost his only daughter to diabetes, which proved to be too much for this now-fragile man.

Me with "Boston Blackie" (Kent Taylor). I helped him stay calm when he sang on stage, until his wife's jealousy put an end to that.

Both of his true loves in life, his singing and his daughter, were taken away from him, and he was never the same.

Kent started down the path of no return. First he stopped his lessons with Barbara, and next he stopped singing altogether. He gave up on life and, six months later, he committed suicide.

Once again Hollywood with its façade of glitz and glamour, hopes and dreams, took its toll.

MY DARLING *CUGINA* (little cousin) Gloria Rovegno, the "hostess with the mostest" at DiMaggio's, always tried to make everyone comfortable.

She was quite proficient at dealing with celebrities, and when they acted up, she put them in their places. She took attitude from no one, let alone stars with big egos, as we found out the night Ann Sothern and her entourage paraded in.

Born Harriette Lake on January 22, 1909, in Valley City, North Dakota, Ann was just as spunky and irrepressible off-screen as on. This night at DiMaggio's she was obviously unhappy with the table where Gloria wanted to seat her party. Instead of politely asking for a change, Ann demanded preferential treatment. "Do you know who I am?" she snapped.

Everyone knew Gloria as the girl with the big beautiful eyes. That day, she flashed them at Ann and stood her ground, but Ann wasn't finished.

"I am Ann Sothern. I want window seating overlooking the wharf, and I want it this minute," she said.

Her haughty attitude was incredible, but Gloria asked, quite nonchalantly, "Do you have a reservation?"

Ann shot her a look that could kill.

"I don't need a reservation," she said.

"At DiMaggio's you do," Gloria replied.

Before Ann could spew out any more demands, my father interceded. He always knew what to say to defuse any situation with grace and to make both sides feel as if each had won the skirmish. For *cugina* Gloria, he had a standard word of advice: "Use kindness as a key to getting around flare-ups with temperamental types." Ann Sothern became putty in his hands, and she returned regularly to DiMaggio's for years.

My personal encounters with Ann proved to be a bit more complex. They also confirmed that she behaved this way with everyone, no matter who they were or what they could do for her.

Ann had been taking vocal coaching from Barbara—and Lord knows, she desperately needed it. Her whiny voice was excellent for comedy, but it always stopped her from making it big in dramatic parts. She visited Barbara not only for voice coaching, but to be counseled spiritually. Barbara reached her students on many levels because of her training in the Church of Religious Science, where she had received a master of science degree in metaphysics.

Barbara really helped Ann to develop a very good singing voice, but to no avail commercially. Ann made a recording that I still have, but it never made the pop charts. At the time, Ann was having major problems, claiming that her managers and others were stealing millions of dollars. She desperately wanted starring roles and had the talent for them, but agents and directors couldn't visualize her playing those parts.

Back then, actresses were controlled by the stupidity and pretense of the Hollywood elite. Powerful men in charge didn't allow women to be their true selves and certainly didn't allow their mental abilities to shine through. Many intelligent women were used and abused by the system, and by society as well.

Marilyn Monroe fit that genre, too, but Marilyn was also putting on an act. And she was good at it—fatally so. While she longed to be a great dramatic actress, the studios saw her only as a sex symbol, nothing more than a face, hips, and breasts to be exploited. Since they made so much money from her physical charms, why portray her any other way and take a chance? If Marilyn wanted her career to continue, she had to be that breathless beauty who appeared not to think at all, but just giggled and jiggled her way across the screen. For a long time she was willing to do just that.

The studios didn't care for Ann Sothern's ambitions either. They saw her as just another actress. They criticized her voice and nagged her about her weight, which was always a problem for her.

Over and over during the years I was in show business, I saw the pressures weighing down on people as they tried to hold onto stardom.

To make ends meet, many performers also modeled. I was no exception.

I suspect similar problems exist for many actresses today. For Ann those frustrations became particularly hard to bear. Yet compared to the general public, she had it all—a cook and assistants who waited on her hand and foot and catered to her every whim. She even had a maid to comb her hair. If the maid were combing her hair, and the phone would ring—only inches away from Ann—she wouldn't pick it up. No, she had the maid answer it for her, as if she were royalty or something.

Yet she was terribly unhappy. Eventually, because of her financial losses, Ann had to sell her Bel Air home. She was a good business-woman, generally speaking, but those around her couldn't be trusted. When she placed her faith in others, her world came crashing down around her. She was beginning to feel like everyone wanted something from her, and she became increasingly despondent. Here was a woman whose star power had peaked but was still living in the past.

Barbara felt that Ann needed someone to listen to her and suggested that I go to stay with her for a while so she would have the company of someone who cared about her but wanted nothing in return. I had reservations, but Barbara knew how to appeal to my soft side. She felt that Ann needed me and finally I relented. Pushing aside all I'd heard about her nasty attitude, I tried to be generous.

At the time, Ann had just finished her run in the movies as blond, wisecracking Maisie. She was in Reno, Nevada, appearing in a play, *Barefoot in the Park*, I believe.

Well, I only lasted three weeks with her, which tells you something. Talk about attitude! She would snap her fingers and expect everybody to jump. Usually they did, and believe me, she always got them to jump to new heights.

In the first few days I was with her, she found out that I wasn't about to fulfill her unbelievable demands. She finally learned the word "No," but didn't like it one bit.

Another problem that added to her woes was that Ann loved sweets, particularly pastries. That sure didn't help her to keep the trim figure she needed for films. For her it was a constant struggle to manage the pounds, which always looked bigger on the screen. She'd go to a fat farm, starve, get cranky, lose weight, then end up making and baking her own pastries for a marathon eating frenzy. She actually ate more than ever, and her weight ballooned with a vengeance.

She wasn't very happy with my company, either, truth be told. I think she wanted a binging companion to make her feel better about her eating habits, but I would not do it. I was a petite woman who didn't much care for sweets. Besides, I was still working in film and television, as well as on stage, and no one wants a tubby ingénue. I had to

Ann Sothern

June 9th 1963

Miss June Di Maggio
c/o Barbara Klein
8561 West Knoll
Los Angeles, 46,California

Dear June:

Just a hasty note to thank you for your nice
letter. Have been rehearsing like mad and sweltering
in the heat. It's really terribly warm!

Thank you so much for looking after the doggies
that day. I understand Jenny fell off the wagon one day
and sister Marian was most inconvenienced. Next fall off,
she's through.

Well, dear, I hope you have found something
that's keeping you happy and I'm enclosing an itinerary
so you and Barbara will know where I am. I called Barbara
one evening and got her exchange. I guess they didn't
tell her to call me back.

Warmest regards, dear,

Ann Sothern

Ann Sothern tried my patience, but we remained friends and exchanged personal notes, such as this one from Ann to me. I even got her to smile when I snapped this picture.

watch my figure, and when I wouldn't eat with her, she fumed. I tried to get her to eat healthy fare, but it was a total waste of time.

A good businesswoman, Ann took me to visit the lovely Dutch community of Solvang, California, because she needed to check on the Hereford cows on her farm. There I was, a city girl quite out of my element, tromping around in the cow patties in my high heels.

On Ann's agenda, food came first. She took me to a quaint little restaurant where, as usual, everyone snapped to attention. She ate up the Swedish meatballs she loved, and she wanted me to chow down the same way. I told her in no uncertain terms that I did not care for any. When I ordered a salad, Ann went ballistic and just about bit my head off with words I won't repeat.

Ann was much older than I was. I was only in my twenties and a little feisty and, yes, a little stinker on occasion. So around that time, I started calling her "Annie," a name I knew she absolutely hated. "Hi, Annie," I'd say, mimicking that whiny voice of hers, and she would get furious. In my defense, she *was* a whiner. Her complaints were too numerous; nothing was ever right.

But Ann had a soft side, too.

I believe she liked me for standing up to her and not taking her guff. She offered Barbara and me her Idaho home for a week to relax away from Tinseltown. We had a wonderful time in that lovely country retreat, which was all decked out in blue and white. Finally she realized there were at least two people in the world, Barbara and me, who wanted nothing from her and were willing to extend a helping hand. She even came to like my calling her Annie, and started calling me by the more endearing "Junie."

Perhaps I hung in for those weeks with Ann because behind all that bravado was a sad lady. Because of my own family's fame, I knew that many celebrities are terribly unhappy. They may have lots of money, enormous houses, and total star power, but they're not immune to sadness. Because they trust those around them to take care of things, they sometimes get burned and then become hardened to life, and their lives end with them having few real friends, if any.

Barbara tried to counsel Ann and others, hoping to give them some solace. She couldn't solve all their problems, but she offered them guidance and gave them tools to cope.

In all she did—bless her heart—Ann tried her best. She even attempted to get her daughter Tisha, by husband Robert Sterling, to take voice and diction classes for a chance at a TV and movie career, but like mother, like daughter. Tisha's voice had that same whiny quality. She was a beautiful girl, but lacked the on-screen presence that her mother possessed. For her, performing was just not meant to be.

Ann went on to play the busybody Susie McNamara in the '50s television series "My Private Secretary" and eventually starred in "The Ann Sothern Show." She and I stayed friends, periodically touching base and catching up on our lives. Ann lived out her final years in Idaho with her daughter and grandkids, where I hope she finally found some peace of mind and happiness.

After all her years of struggle, she finally received her first Academy Award nomination at the age of seventy-nine for *The Whales of August.* After seventy years in show business, Ann Sothern died of heart failure in 2001 at age ninety-two.

❦

MEANWHILE, I WAS ESTABLISHING my stage career, and Barbara's career blossomed as a vocal coach to the stars. I got to meet Jeanette MacDonald yet again when she became Barbara's student for both her voice and spiritual counseling.

To June Bug
from your Gemini Juettur
with fond regards
Jeanette MacDonald

JEANETTE
MAC DONALD

This is the Jeanette MacDonald I remember. I was
just that little girl who reached out for her and the
stage. I know I was always her "June Bug," too.

Jeanette MacDonald influenced my life as a performer, but she also taught me by example how to be caring to others (such as in this handwritten note).

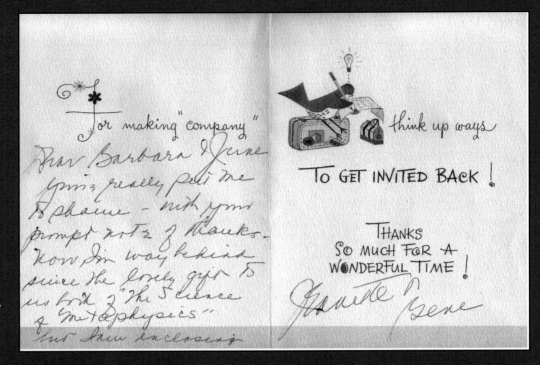

Dear Barbara and June,

You've really put me to shame—with your prompt note of thanks. Now I'm way behind since the lovely gift to us both of "The Science of Metaphysics." But I am enclosing the "Food Pilot." It is so like mine it's almost as tho they copied their ideas—or at least exchanged them. Now a final word of thanks to you for the evening together. Will do it again. Gene joins me in love.

Jeanette

Dear Barbara
        and June Bug

Last nite was like Thanksgiving with the lovely basket of goodies And I am certainly thankful to you for your thoughtfulness and the happiness your presence brought to us all. I enjoyed the evening

and I had the happy feeling everyone else did, too — the nicest feeling a hostess can have. I slept like a baby, a rarity for me and I think the warm atmosphere of the evening was the answer. So many thanks for coming — Love Jeanette

I was always thrilled to hear from Jeanette MacDonald —she sent the cutest notes. She was such a darling, and she always appreciated it when Barbara and I did anything for her.

Dear Barbara and June Bug,

Last night was like Thanksgiving with the lovely basket of goodies and I am certainly thankful to you for your thoughtfulness and the happiness your presence brought to us all. I enoyed the evening and I had the happy feeling everyone else did too. The nicest feeling a hostess can have. I slept like a baby, a rarity for me and I think the warm atmosphere of the evening was the answer. So many thanks for coming.

Love,
Jeanette

Jeanette was married to Gene Raymond, who loved her very much and who also came to Barbara to learn metaphysics. An actor in his own right, he wrote many love songs for Jeanette's repertoire and accompanied her on many appearances. I remember him as such a gentleman—quiet, sweet, and totally devoted to Jeanette. When Jeanette died, Gene was devastated and turned to Barbara to help him deal with her passing. But I'm getting ahead of myself.

When Jeanette became one of Barbara's students, I couldn't resist the temptation to ask—no, plead—with Barbara to invite Jeanette and Gene over for dinner. To my amazement, Jeanette accepted. I was so excited that I didn't know where to begin. I wanted everything to be absolutely perfect, and the farmer's market seemed my logical first stop for the best of everything. Something told me to buy a lot of fruit. I can still remember using my last eighteen bucks to buy every fresh fruit they had, along with all the dinner fixings. In those days, $18 went a long way, and I knew it would be worth it.

The following day I scurried around the kitchen preparing the finest Italian dinner I could, using every skill I possessed. At 7 P.M. exactly the doorbell rang, and there in my living room stood the woman I had idolized for so many years. I was beside myself. After all, this was the first time I'd seen her since that chance encounter when I was just a little girl. All I could say was a rapid-fire "Hi! Hi! Hi!" Silly, I knew, but I couldn't help myself.

Gene was with her, as always, and they had boxes with them that Jeanette handed to me. As I opened them, she explained that she had heard I was Swiss-Italian. Inside were beer steins she had bought in Germany and Switzerland on her many travels.

"I wanted you to have them, June Bug," she told me.

I was stunned.

Obviously, Barbara must have filled her in on my lineage and pet name and explained what she meant to me, but never did I expect she would be so caring as to bring me these treasures. I still display those steins, and every time I look at them I see her beautiful face and recall her sweet voice saying, "I hope you like them, June Bug." She never called me anything else after that.

But disappointment loomed.

"Everything smells so great, but I'm on a diet and all I can eat is liver, carrot juice, and fruit," Jeanette said. "Don't worry, because Gene can eat my portion."

She'd even brought her own liver and carrot juice so as not to cause problems.

At first I was devastated. I had cooked the whole day and now she couldn't even taste what I had prepared to perfection. I wanted to please her, of course, so I took the raw liver she had brought with her and baked it, because our broiler wasn't working.

Pouring her carrot juice, I remembered I'd bought all that fruit. At the market, my intuition—an ability that would pop up for me time and again—had rung true.

I piled every piece of that fresh fruit I had borne home—apples, grapes, plums, pineapple, and more—on a plate. I was thrilled to see her eat it all with much appreciation.

Of all the stars I knew in my lifetime in the business, Jeanette MacDonald was the only one who didn't have emotional and mental problems. She was a genuine, loving person, untainted by Hollywood.

As we enjoyed our respective dinners, Jeanette turned to me and said, "You're that bright little penny I held on to at the San Francisco Opera House, aren't you?" I couldn't believe that she had remembered that incident after all those years, yet she had.

We talked until the wee hours. She told me how it all began for her as a showgirl, a dancer on Broadway, and how she beat out other starlets for musicals because she could sing so beautifully. She told me what doing screen tests was like and gave me tips. She explained to me that her wonderful voice was small compared to others. Jeanette was a lyric soprano, which was perfect for her career because at the time studios didn't want huge voices, preferring amplification to do the job. It was the quality of her voice that was so superior.

She told us stories about her father, the minister, who held séances. When it came to clients hearing "spirits" speak, Jeanette admitted it was she who provided those eerie voices from beyond—from beyond the drapes, that is. She explained that it might not have been the right thing to do, but she was only a child, and that was a different day and age.

After dinner, Gene played the piano, Jeanette sang, and I was totally entranced. Gene played songs he had written for her, and all was going perfectly for me until Jeanette turned and said, "Barbara tells me you sing, June Bug. Won't you sing with me?"

The magic was broken! "I can't sing," I sputtered. "I'm too nervous."

"I understand the first song you heard of mine was 'Ah, Sweet Mystery of Life,'" Jeanette said. She saw how very nervous I was, so she gently held my hand and sang that song just for me. Then I joined in and sang with her!

Hearing Jeanette MacDonald sing for me in my own home was a spiritual experience. From that moment on we became great friends.

6

NO MORE DUCK FOR MARILYN MONROE

THE STORY OF MARILYN and Joe is the stuff fairy tales and Hollywood romances are made of, but my uncle should never have married a major star like Marilyn Monroe. Joe came from a different world than Marilyn did, just as he had with his first wife, Dorothy Arnold.

His destiny may have been to cross with Marilyn's, but not permanently. By the time they met, he was past his prime and semiretired. Marilyn was shooting the movie *Monkey Business* when her agent arranged for her to meet Joe for a dinner date.

The agent had dreamed up the whole thing, and Marilyn was just playing along, but Joe was looking forward to seeing the beautiful woman he'd so admired. He was used to everyone adoring him and felt confident that she'd be impressed with all his achievements.

The truth was, the baseball diamond wasn't that girl's best friend. Imagine his shock upon learning that Marilyn had no interest in baseball and no clue who he—the great Joe DiMaggio—was. This gorgeous movie star didn't care about the game, much less the international fame of one of its best-known players. Plus, he was thirty-seven and she was twenty-five. Yet they fell head over heels in love. They had the kind of chemistry that comes once in a lifetime and, for some, never.

Joe was still living in San Francisco when he called me to say that he was planning to visit Barbie and me in Beverly Hills. He and Marilyn were engaged, and this would be our very first meeting with Joe's famous fiancée.

I realize that when people hear the DiMaggio name the first thing that pops into their minds is baseball, but Uncle Joe had hobbies aside from the game, and one of them was duck hunting with my father in the marshes.

I'm not sure if it was the sport of it or if he really liked the taste of roast wild duck; maybe it was a little of both. On this particular hunting excursion, Joe came all the way from San Francisco to Beverly Hills with a treat for his bride-to-be—four ducks, two small teals, and two mammoths. He wanted to invite Marilyn so that she could taste the birds he'd bagged, and he asked me if I'd prepare them.

I knew how important it was for Joe to please his sweetheart, or maybe to impress her. It's a guy thing, after all, for the skillful hunter to go out and make a good catch for his woman. Since Joe couldn't impress Marilyn with his prowess on the baseball diamond, maybe he thought his hunting skills could wow her.

However, behind Joe's request was some cunning. Unless one knows how to prepare the birds, they taste less than savory. Fortunately, cooking was one of my passions, and I was always glad to whip up tasty dishes for Joe between my stints at the studio.

Even so, wild ducks are a delicacy and an acquired taste. Their meat has a gray look to it and tastes gamey, so anyone who has not grown accustomed to the flavor can be less than enchanted with it.

That's why preparation is very important. Joe knew I could cook the birds properly by first stuffing them with apple, onion, and celery and then baking them for forty minutes.

When he arrived with Marilyn, she was talking up a storm. I didn't make much of it. Yes, it was Marilyn, but she was just starting out as an actress like I was, so I wasn't bowled over when I opened the door and there she stood. At first I thought she might be nervous as she chattered away, but later I learned that Marilyn just loved to talk. On the other hand, Joe hardly spoke a word when he was around her. He was not the type to hold hands and kiss much in public, but I do remember him showing affection to Marilyn many times when he visited my parents. I think sometimes that he was so much in awe of her that he didn't know what to do. What a match!

RIGHT AWAY I FELT as if I had known Marilyn for years. It didn't hurt that we were both Geminis. Our birthdays were just days apart and our personalities were so similar that I think we had the connection of the Gemini twins. We struck up a conversation that never seemed to end, even long after she and Joe went their separate ways. We chatted about literature, about concepts and philosophy and about the business of show business. All in all, though, we were basically like girls regardless of our chronological ages. Marilyn could get me to do the darnedest things, even against my better judgment. In the years that followed, we talked about religion and the seamy side of Hollywood, but we did fun girly things, too, and, boy, did we laugh a lot, telling jokes and giggling in the strangest of situations. I just wish she could have lived to find true happiness the way I did, but that was not to be.

Our conversations were completely natural, and Marilyn didn't talk a whole lot about her work. She did ask Barbara about her metaphysical practice and counseling. Marilyn was fascinated by Barbara's spiritual work.

Barbara was careful when she talked about her work because privacy for her clients—many of whom were famous—was always paramount. When she counseled anyone, including Marilyn, the conversation was between the two of them and no one else. No tapes, no photos, no transcripts were ever made in order to give her star clients security that their thoughts and feelings would be kept secret. When the dinner conversation turned to Marilyn's work at the studio, she said that she didn't like being called a sexpot and that she really wanted to be known for her acting ability.

For Joe there had been plenty of women along the way, but this one was special. Not simply because she was an icon, but because she was extraordinary on the inside, too. Maybe it was my extrasensory perception (ESP) at work, but I knew that this was more than a passing relationship for my uncle and Marilyn Monroe.

At that first dinner, Joe was naturally proud and excited that we'd be eating *his* wild ducks on this special occasion, but when Marilyn heard what we'd be serving, she got serious and adorably concerned. Before dinner began, she cornered me in the kitchen.

"June," she said, "I've never eaten wild ducks before. What if I don't like them? I don't want to hurt Joe's feelings."

I told her not to worry, and we agreed on a signal.

"If you don't like the taste, turn to me and give me *the look*," I said, crossing my eyes.

Marilyn did the same. It was all I could do to not to burst out laughing.

I let Barbara know what we had in store so that there would be no slip-ups. We decided that if Marilyn gave the signal, Barbara and I would engage Joe in conversation. Then, while Barbara kept him busy, I would take Marilyn's plate away on the pretense of getting her more wild rice from the kitchen, and there I could substitute something more to her liking.

Dinner began. Joe, sitting at the head of the table and beaming from ear to ear, sliced the tiny breasts from the tender young teals and proudly placed them on Marilyn's plate along with a small mound of rice. I could see how much this meant to him: He so wanted Marilyn to be pleased with his catch.

She sweetly smiled at Joe, took a hearty bite of the duck, and all the color drained from her face. She turned almost as gray as the duck, but, not wanting to give away her disgust, she kept chewing vigorously to keep from having to taste it. Of course, Joe thought that she found his birds absolutely delicious.

This all transpired in a split second. Marilyn turned to me as quickly as she dared and, facing away from Joe, crossed her eyes and curled up her nose all at once. I flew into action while Barbara began engaging Joe in conversation.

I scooped up Marilyn's plate and, without missing a beat, said, "Oh, Marilyn, you need more wild rice. Let me get it." Plate in hand, stifling my laughter, I retreated to the kitchen.

I scooted a waiting hamburger onto her plate and smothered it in wild rice so that no one else could see what was underneath. I hoped that Joe would assume that Marilyn relished the duck he'd shot and all would be right with their world.

I placed the new delicacy in front of Marilyn. She tasted it and smiled broadly.

"This is just wonderful!" she purred.

She went on to praise Joe for his hunting prowess, and that made him swell with pride. I was tickled that we had pulled it off. Joe never knew the difference. He saw Marilyn's empty plate and told her he was glad she was so taken with wild duck.

"Maybe I'll shoot some more for you again soon," he said.

Marilyn must have decided that she wasn't going through this whole charade a second time. We got away with it once, but didn't want to risk an instant replay and hurt Joe's feelings.

"I really enjoyed the duck, Joe, but I don't think I want it again," she said, looking him right in the eye.

The way she said it, in that breathy, sexy, coy voice of hers, there was no way any man could have been crestfallen. Joe certainly wasn't.

Before she left that evening of our first meeting, Marilyn put her arms around me and said, "Junie, you're a real friend."

I don't know whether she realized it, but her words were to predict our forthcoming bond. We developed a real closeness all too rare in Hollywood, where illusion always trumps reality. Marilyn understood the value of family and friends and the simpler things in life, perhaps because these were the very things she longed for the most.

Before she left, she picked up our Burmese cat, named Minka Ty Sing, and stroked her. Minka fell in love with Marilyn that night and gently nudged her head under Marilyn's chin. The bond between the so-called sex kitten and our beloved Burmese continued whenever Marilyn came to visit.

7

matchmaking, musicals, and another barbara

SHORTLY AFTER JOE brought Marilyn to visit, he tried to play matchmaker for me. I was about twenty-three years old and, from an Italian viewpoint, getting a little old for marriage. By this time most of my friends were married and had at least a couple of kids. Joe knew many eligible men, most of them athletes. He told me about Poochie, a football hero he knew, who he thought would be perfect for me.

I didn't care for blind dates, but I wanted to please Joe. He nagged me until I finally gave in. After all, he was only thinking of his niece's future.

That night I got all dolled up. I had dated some of the most handsome men in Hollywood, including royalty like Baron Sepy Dubronyi. When Poochie rang the bell and I opened the door, I just stood there for a moment, speechless, not prepared for the man—or should I say structure—before me. He seemed to have no neck, just a head on his immense shoulders. At 5'2½" tall, I felt like a pygmy in a land of giants, but I had promised Joe I'd go out with him, and I intended to keep my word. He didn't talk much; he sort of grunted. When he did speak, it was about—you guessed it—football. What I knew about the game you could fit in a thimble, so I was bored out of my skull the whole evening.

I'm sure he was, too. When I talked about show business, all I got was quizzical looks. Even when I mentioned box-office stars, he had no clue who I was talking about, and I was clueless when he talked about his teammates, so we were even.

We called it an early evening, but the next day I thanked Joe for trying to bring romance into my life. Still, I was adamant about not letting anyone—not even the great Joe DiMaggio—run my love life. I didn't want him to feel badly, however. He had tried, even if it had been a mistake, so I told him a white lie and put a positive spin on the evening with Poochie.

That was my mistake because Joe said quickly, "I know this baseball player who would be perfect for you."

I honestly didn't know who Mickey Mantle was, and didn't care, and I gave Joe a look that stopped him in his tracks. That was the end of his matchmaking, as much as I appreciated him for caring.

To outsiders Hollywood may have looked glamorous and exciting, but on the inside it was fraught with pain and anguish. Perhaps it wasn't the actual fame that starry-eyed actors sought as much as it was solace and love, but so often they sought it in all the wrong places—from beds to bars. In all the years I worked in the business, the only happy star I knew was the lovely Jeanette MacDonald and her wonderful husband, Gene Raymond.

During my short but fascinating career in La-La Land, I had my run-ins with the rich and famous and infamous. From comic actresses like Eve Arden and Ann Sothern to the legendary architect Frank Lloyd Wright, they were like sad, lost souls seeking peace and contentment in a mixed-up world. As a result, many of them came to Barbara Klein's studio for voice coaching and spiritual counseling.

Barbara was adamant about protecting their privacy, and that, as I've said, included not taking any photographs. Barbara and my mother both felt it was rude to take snapshots of star friends when they didn't look or feel their best. They had enough photos taken by paparazzi and movie studios. What they needed was a place of solace, which they found at our apartment and in my parents' home.

I GOT TO KNOW Barbara Stanwyck in 1952 when she and Marilyn worked on the film *Clash by Night.* She was always so thoughtful. I treasure her handwritten letters thanking me for the candles I gave her for Christmas in 1953 and the note she sent me when I wanted to share some wild ducks that Joe hunted the following January. Her husband-—"Mr. Taylor," as she called him—was also a duck hunter. Barbara admitted that she hadn't acquired a taste for duck and could never eat them.

After our first encounter, it would be several years before I would see Barbara again, but see her I would.

SOME YEARS EARLIER, the great producer duo of Russell Lewis and Howard Young had been impressed by my 1949 performance in *Dear Virtue,* and they signed me to do the first of eleven musicals in 1952, the second year of Music Circus, their summer stock theater in Sacramento. I went on to perform in the only opera ever produced at Music Circus, *Die Fliedermaus,* with the great Metropolitan Opera star Virginia MacWaters. They teamed us together because I could sing the classics as well as musical comedy. Once again, I have Barbara Klein to thank for the ability to switch back and forth with such ease.

Lewis and Young remained my great friends until their passing. Music Circus is the last of its era today, but it's still going strong under the managing direction of Russell's son, Richard Lewis.

A whirlwind occurred in my career when "Look" magazine published a spread entitled "Theater-on-the-Run," featuring me at Music Circus on August 26, 1952. I appeared in eleven shows at Music Circus.

Posing for a mug shot was no problem for
"yours truly" at the hot summer rehearsals in
Sacramento, California, under the
Music Circus tent.

Rehearsals under the tent at Music Circus in the summer were grueling, but the audiences always gave me energy.

Sexy bedroom eyes made my performance a memorable one in "Firefly" at Music Circus.

"Sadly! Look at me
I'm here! Your Adele.
To June Alpins — most
One of the Talented — adorable
sisters I've ever had in "Fledermaus".
With love,
Virginia MacWatters

"Die Fliedermaus" was the only opera at Music Circus. To
have the compliment of a lifetime from the Metropolitan
Opera's Virginia MacWaters, was a real thrill. (That's me,

8

MORE ABOUT MARILEE

My parents had a gorgeous apartment overlooking the San Francisco Marina green. A large circular window framed Alcatraz across the bay—at least when the fog wasn't settled in. Whenever Uncle Joe and Marilyn came over, he would automatically head for the TV and watch it with my father so that they could digest the news and discuss the day's events.

Marilyn, on the other hand, loved to spend time with Mother, so off to the tiny kitchen they would go, chattering happily about this and that. Marilee actually loved being in the kitchen and never thought of it as work. It was a joy to behold her scurrying around, enjoying the chance to relax. I think she relished the warm feeling of family, particularly in Mother's kitchen, the heart of our home.

There was a soft simplicity about Marilee. She loved poetry and the smell of lavender and was very feminine, yet I was constantly amazed at how down-to-earth she really was. Whenever she came to my parents' home for dinner, she always asked what she could do to help. While Joe and Father watched television in the living room, Marilee studied Mother's actions in that tiny kitchen. She loved doing homey, seemingly mundane tasks and soaked in how to do everything that made a house a home.

Since there were no automatic dishwashers back then, I washed and Marilee dried. When drying forks, she actually pulled the dish-towel between each tine. Sure it was odd, but we never said anything because she was trying so hard to be perfect.

75

My parents, Lee and Tom DiMaggio, lived in this lovely apartment overlooking the Marina green. You could see Alcatraz from their living room.

Everything she did, she did with gusto. Mother often warned her to wear rubber gloves to protect her lovely hands, but Marilee didn't care if her hands got dried and chafed. She would plunge right into the hot dishwater, seeming to enjoy the sensation.

With all Marilyn's work on the set, her time was limited and there were many household chores that she never learned how to do. She always tried so hard to please Joe, but no one had taught her how to cook. She learned all the homey stuff from my mother, who taught her to make boiled beef for him, a dish he loved. She even taught Marilyn how to cook a great spaghetti sauce in twenty minutes.

Marilee loved the feeling of home and adored my mother, who thought of her as a daughter. Whenever she was with us, I could see the serenity on her face. For those brief moments she wasn't worrying about her career. She didn't have to fret about how she looked, or what she said, or how she behaved; she could just be herself.

Marilee found great comfort in my mother, who sensed her need for someone to believe in and confide in. Mother treated her like family, and in return Marilyn shared her innermost being, her true nature, her dreams. From my mother she received wise counseling and unconditional love.

Marilee never got that kind of comfort from Joe. He just didn't have it in him to help her with that part of her life, no matter how much he loved her; and love her he did to his dying day.

Marilee and I enjoyed entertaining girl talk, and we shared similar experiences. Sometimes we'd vent our frustrations about our lives and loves and Hollywood, often giggling like the young girls we still were. Marilyn loved to laugh, and her sense of humor in real life carried over into her fine comedic timing on the silver screen. I cherish our heart-to-hearts even now.

Marilyn caught me by surprise when she snapped this photo at my mother's house in 1958.

UNCLE JOE LIVED ON Beach Street in the Marina, only three or four blocks away from my parents. Aunt Marie, who took care of Joe's apartment, was a darling yet serious person. Today I guess she'd be diagnosed as obsessive-compulsive. She kept Joe's apartment spotless. Aunt Marie even put a cozy on the doorknob to keep it clean. No one could ever be neat enough for Aunt Marie.

Marilyn liked her, but not her never-spill-anything mentality. That was another reason Marilyn loved to visit Mother, who could care less if there was a little dust bunny or two around. Whenever she visited, she'd make an obligatory stop at Joe's apartment and pay her respects to Aunt Marie, then grab her fur coat and make her escape to see my mother and father. They lived on the second floor. When Marilyn pressed the button in the lobby, Mother buzzed her in and she hurried up the stairs.

On the third floor above my parents lived a neighbor who was very prim and proper. Never a hair out of place, her clothes were always starched and straight. This lady knew only that the DiMaggios lived below her, but little else about what went on in my parents' apartment.

One day she was on her way downstairs just as Marilyn was coming up. With flawless timing, they met in front of my parents' apartment door. You can imagine the neighbor's reaction at coming face to face with Marilyn Monroe. The woman was in a state of shock, struck speechless. The only sound was Marilee, an amused smile on her face, rapping on my parents' door. When Mother opened it, out flew Tommy, my mother's cockatiel, who loved Marilyn and spent every minute with her when she came to visit.

Tommy couldn't pronounce the "J" in my name, so he would always call me "Lunie." Mother had taught Tommy to say Marilyn's name, too. When she came over, he headed straight for her and landed on top of her

My mother absolutely adored that cockatiel of hers (the same one Marilyn teased the neighbor with by saying it was "her son"). And Tommy sure loved her too.

head, repeating "Mari-lyn-Mon-roe, Mari-lyn-Mon-roe" over and over, and then gave a whistle that could be heard two floors down.

Not missing a beat this one day, Marilee turned to the poor woman, who was frozen to the spot.

"It's okay," she said with a straight face, Tommy still perched atop her head. "This is my son and he's here to greet me."

With that, she glided into the apartment.

Marilyn loved all kinds of animals, so she also gave lots of attention to our dog Pedy. Now that I think about it, I think Marilee craved affection wherever she could find it, and what better source than from a family pet who asked nothing more than to be loved back?

AFTER FINISHING A MOVIE in Hollywood, Marilyn would come to San Francisco to stay with Joe. However, Joe frequently went out for a massage or to the yacht club, often for hours at a time, so Marilyn would dash around the corner to my folks' apartment.

For one memorable dinner, Father created an especially savory seafood dish that became very popular at DiMaggio's—a baked cioppino with clams, lobster, prawns, crab, and halibut. I have tried to find a baked cioppino recipe elsewhere, but the dish seems to have faded into culinary history.

My father also created one of the most famous dishes the restaurant served, Lobster Thermador, made with fresh tomatoes, Tillamook cheese, and his secret ingredient, beer. Placing it under the broiler for just three minutes treated you to palate-pleasing perfection.

Whenever Marilyn came to visit, Mother would call my father at the restaurant and say, "Marilyn's here! She's staying for dinner, so bring home Lobster Thermador." Despite—or perhaps due to—its yummy taste, Marilyn learned to be careful of her lobster intake. After one visit home, I brought some Lobster Thermador with me back to Beverly Hills. I called Marilyn and she came by in a minute. She ate it all, but then she got worried. She had an early stage call the next morning and fretted that the camera would show the succulent lobster clawing at her hips. It didn't, of course.

❦

WHENEVER I HAD TIME off from one of my shows, I always went to visit my parents in the City. On one particular visit on my birthday—as I've said, just a few days away from Marilee's—she happened to be in San Francisco, too. Marilee and I were deep in conversation about the shows we were doing when Father came home from the restaurant and mentioned that he'd be going deep-sea fishing the next day. Her eyes lit up.

Our conversation ended rather abruptly, and in that soft voice of hers she cooed, "I've never been deep-sea fishing before, and I'd love to go."

As a commercial fisherman, Father never lost the love of going out on the *Yankee Clipper* to catch fresh fish for the restaurant. I used to wonder if he took the *Clipper* out to snare the catch of the day or to be out on the open sea. Joe loved being out there with him, too, enjoying a day away from San Francisco's hustle and bustle.

Marilee was excited about going fishing, and when she wanted something, she knew how to work the males in the room to get it. I was laughing to myself at how she was going to get her way when she turned to me for support with those wide eyes.

"Don't look at me, Marilee," I said. "I get seasick." We had no seasick patches in those days, and I used to get sick to my stomach before we even sailed under the Golden Gate Bridge, but Marilee wasn't about to give in.

"Come on, Junie, be a good sport," she said.

Father backed her up.

"Just eat a lot of crackers and you'll be fine."

I knew better, but their insistence wore me down. I suspected that I'd live to regret it, but didn't realize that so would Marilee.

She could hardly contain her enthusiasm. That night she slept over, but she was so filled with anticipation about going out on the boat early the next morning that she couldn't get to sleep. I wasn't too thrilled about getting up in the wee hours and finally had to tell her that if we didn't get some shut-eye, we wouldn't make it out to the *Clipper*.

At 4:00 A.M. she jumped out of bed, eager for her deep-sea debut. When shooting a movie, I had to get up in the middle of the night, but for me, getting up before the birds was *for* the birds.

Marilee, however, was chipper as a spring robin and raring to go. She was more accustomed to making movies than I was and no stranger to early morning calls. I did more stage work, which called for evening performances. I made sure that Marilee knew that I was going along with this adventure just for her and that she owed me big time.

It seemed that nothing was going to dampen Marilee's enthusiasm for this excursion. She hadn't brought any of her own clothes, so I loaned her a pair of my white duck pants. On her they looked more like a pair of Capri pants because she was taller than I was. She also wore a pair of my prescription sunglasses, which were not quite as strong as hers, but they helped some.

When we were ready, Uncle Joe joined us. Like a little girl promised her first pony ride, Marilyn was so excited she couldn't stop chattering, but by the time we got to the dock, the fog had moved in. It wasn't just dark; it was cold, damp, and dreary. A sense of foreboding came over me, and I was ready to head back to the snug bed I didn't want to leave in the first place, while Marilee was bright and cheery, bouncing around as if it were a bright spring morning.

I couldn't believe that she didn't feel the cold as I did, but I wanted to make her happy, so with me shivering, we shoved off for a saga neither of us would soon forget. We headed under the Golden Gate Bridge to where the salmon were plentiful. Dark waves splashed up against the side of the boat, which was rocking up and down, up and down, up and down, while my stomach did the same.

Suddenly, Marilee's enthusiasm waned. She went silent and turned to me with those big baby-blue eyes—a bit watery by now.

"Got any crackers, Junie?" she asked.

So we ate crackers, lots of them, but the more we ate, the sicker we felt. Meanwhile, Father and Joe were having a wonderful time. I doubt that they cared any longer about what they might reel in. We had become their morning's entertainment. There they were, laughing at us as we spent most of the day bent over the side of the boat upchucking crackers.

The fishy smell alone was enough to make us want to perish on the spot.

"Marilee, this is all your fault," I couldn't resist telling her. "I knew this would happen. Now give me another cracker!"

Weakly she pointed a finger back at me, silently accusing me of not warning her of the perils of deep-sea fishing.

By the time we returned to the dock, Joe and my father had to practically carry us off the boat. The two of us crawled up the stairs to my parents' apartment, scrambling to the bathrooms.

I thought we'd never come out again. After what seemed forever, bringing up every cracker we'd downed and then some, we looked to Mother for help, but about all she could do was offer us milk and crackers all over again. Then she told us to lie down before we fell down.

Marilee lay on one end of my parents' huge bed, and I collapsed on the other. The room was spinning. We moaned and groaned, two sick girls begging to be put out of our misery. We were as pale as the white sheets we snuggled up in. Dying had to be better than this.

Mother got a big kick out of our predicament, which didn't offer us much comfort. She had a wicked sense of humor, another reason why Marilyn loved her. Later, knowing that we hadn't eaten the entire day, Mother brought us some beef broth to settle our stomachs, but nothing seemed to help. Back to the bathrooms we flew. Sleep was the only solution left.

At about 2:00 in the morning, my eyes suddenly popped open. I looked over at Marilee. She had a strange look on her face.

"What's that odor?" she asked "It's making me sick all over again."

I smelled it, too, but couldn't imagine where it was coming from until a swinging motion above our heads caught our attention. On the light fixture directly above us my prankster mother had dangled a piece of fried chicken.

She heard us talking, came into the room and asked, "Would you two like a bowl of chicken soup now?"

Need I tell you where Marilee and I spent the next few hours—again?

Later that morning we began to feel better. Marilee told Mother she was starting to get her appetite back.

"And what will Tom be bringing home for supper from DiMaggio's?" she asked

I saw that glint in my mother's eye. With a straight face she said, "Salmon, of course!"

Marilee and I never went deep-sea fishing again, and I never let her forget that time she'd convinced me to go along in the first place.

9

THE BIRTHDAY GUEST

MARILYN CONSTANTLY FEARED gaining too much weight, since the big screen made certain parts of the body seem larger, but she loved to eat. I can't remember her ever exercising, and she had a very healthy appetite, so the problem seemed to compound itself.

An Italian birthday is a full-blown bash with food, drink, song, and lots of joke telling and laughter. After our one-time fishing expedition ended in disaster, Joe brought Marilyn to my father's birthday party. She fit in beautifully with the singing and story telling.

My family was accustomed to rubbing elbows with celebrities, so everyone at the party treated her like one of us, but this was a new experience for Marilyn. Suddenly she was part of a sizable Italian family that loved life and lived it to the max.

She brought Father a tackle box and, childlike again, clearly hoped that he would like her birthday gift.

"I know you must have so many," she told him hopefully, "but I thought you could always use an extra one."

Father knew how to make people feel good. He fussed over that tackle box as if were it exactly what he'd been hoping for, and it delighted me to see the pride on Marilyn's face.

She fit right in and was having a great time eating to her heart's content and, I fear, indulging a bit too much in Annie Rudie's lasagna. Then she called me aside. I couldn't imagine what she wanted to talk about, but I could tell she wanted it very hush-hush.

"Junie," she whispered. "I can't breathe. I ate too much lasagna, and I feel like I'm suffocating in this girdle. Can I go somewhere and take it off?"

I nearly burst out laughing. "Sure, Marilee. Get comfortable!"

She slipped away to free herself of her restraint. Moments later, she returned looking relieved, happy as could be, and ready to down more of the feast.

I know that you've likely heard stories that Marilyn was an alcoholic, but all I ever saw her drink was a glass of sherry on special occasions. Even at that birthday party for my father, when everyone else was drinking and having a great time, all Marilyn sipped was a single glass of sherry. Perhaps the only time she may have had too much was when she could no longer stand the ugliness of Hollywood's bright lights.

Our parties never got out of hand, but everyone was having a wonderful time. Once again, Marilyn proved herself a good sport with a sense of humor. I can't recall whether she or I had the idea first, but we both thought it would be great fun to play a prank on Father, the birthday boy.

By this time he had enjoyed a few glasses of wine. He wasn't drunk, but he had developed what used to be called "quite a toot" and was one happy fellow. So, giggling and conspiring, Marilyn and I slunk away to retrieve the girdle she had taken off a while earlier. We managed to get him to shimmy into it over his trousers. Feeling no pain, he went along with the prank. Marilyn was howling at the sight, and Mother couldn't stop laughing. I had the presence of mind to snap a picture for posterity and got a shot of this trio, but just barely, since I was in hysterics, too.

UNCLE JOE WAS ALWAYS very quiet. I suspect that was what made him so successful in his career. Not one to joke around, he was able to

Father's Birthday Party, 1954

Marilyn was so proud to present my father with a tackle box for his birthday at my parents' apartment. Here, my father and mother make a big fuss about how lovely a gift it was.

Just look at the happiness on Marilyn's face as my father holds the tackle box. She was like a big kid, delighted that he loved what she picked out. Her smile could light up the room.

Marilyn loved being with my family and joined us whenever she could. On the other hand, my Uncle Joe was still kind of a loner, even with a movie star on his arm.

What a sport! Who else but Marilyn Monroe could pull off the stunt of getting her girdle on my father? (It was a big relief for her, too, after all that lasagna!) Marilyn had a good laugh too!

The times Marilyn and Joe cuddled, I can only guess what little secrets they shared. I loved seeing them when their love was still so special. I wish they could have sustained that love, but it was not meant to be.

concentrate on baseball, but Marilyn needed relief from the stress of being under the microscope, so she turned to my chatty mother, who always had a joke or two. Marilee enjoyed them, no matter how corny they were. To entertain her, Mother would get into high gear, accents and all.

Marilee would sit there, enthralled by Mother's joke telling.

"There was this Jewish man," Mother once began, "who lived across the street from this Italian. The Jewish man had five children and the Italian man had none. The Italian opened his window one morning and asked Ike, 'How come you have so many children and I, a big, strapping Italian, have none?'

"Ike told him," Mother continued in her best Jewish accent "'You should dab perfume all over your wife and open the window.'"

"'Okay,' said the Italian man. 'And then what?'"

"'Just whistle for me, and I'll be right over.'"

Marilyn was in hysterics. She could listen for hours to Mother's jokes and stories about life. The Marilee I knew loved to tell jokes, too, although she would sometimes forget the punch lines.

She would try to tell a story, but for some reason it would slip her mind. No matter. Not missing a beat, she let her self-deprecating humor take over and snickered at herself with that wonderful giggle that made me laugh harder than if she had remembered how the joke was supposed to turn out.

Sometimes at the end of a joke Marilee would drop her voice very low to make it sound heavy and masculine, which made me laugh even more. By the way, that sexy high-pitched voice she used on screen was just that, a screen voice. Her speaking voice was as normal as any other woman's, but she could turn on that sultry voice whenever she needed to. It was ironic that Marilee found Mother's Italian father joke so funny.

Marilyn would sometimes share intimate information with me without my asking. She told me that she had had a hysterectomy at age sixteen, but didn't elaborate on what condition caused it. What reason would she have to lie to me about such a thing? I know there's much controversy over this, but this is what she told me. When I asked Mother about that part of Marilyn's life, all she said was, "Don't believe everything you hear from outsiders." It was good advice, which I follow to this day.

Some people will make up any story they like to grab readers' attention, such as the one about Marilyn having had a secret son. Not very likely, but Marilyn did love children and lamented not being able to have any of her own.

When she spoke of her own mother, Marilee painted a picture of a troubled woman who had to contend with her own mental problems—to her child's detriment. She knew that her mother was not cruel or uncaring, but very ill, and she never held that against her. Throughout her life, Marilyn took care of all her mother's bills and left provisions after her death to ensure that her mother would be cared for as long as she lived.

She never knew her father. Having grown up without the love of a mother and never having had a real father, the agonizing feeling that no one cared about her must have preyed on Marilee's mind. It saddened her that she never had the love of a real family—something she sought all her life. She desperately needed to be loved, but couldn't trust anyone around her. Marilyn had much baggage in her young life. And then she became a star.

Any actress would love the acting, the glamour, the attention, but most may not have had so many haunting personal questions. Was she loved for herself, Norma Jeane Baker, or as the woman people saw on the screen? Was it affection or lust?

To that question add the overwhelming anxiety that somewhere along the way her heredity might catch up with her. Might she go insane like her mother and wind up in an institution? Because her mother had severe mental illness, Marilyn was tortured by the possibility that she, too, could have mental problems.

It's not fair for any girl to start out with two strikes against her, but Norma Jeane had three—her mother, her father, and her career.

ONE DAY WHEN SHE and Joe were visiting my parents, Joe and my father were watching the news on TV while Marilee and I were in the kitchen helping Mother with dinner. We were preparing boiled beef again. Marilyn was absorbed in learning how to prepare it just the way my mother did, and she was determined to get it right. I wouldn't have been surprised if she'd taken notes.

All of a sudden Joe called, "Marilyn, come quick! There's something about you on TV."

As she walked into the living room, the TV cut to a reporter broadcasting live from New York's La Guardia Airport who was announcing the arrival of the one-and-only Marilyn Monroe on the heels of a member of a prominent East Coast political family. Marilee stood there, stunned. I thought she would just chalk it up to publicity seekers until she turned to me with tears welling in her eyes. I'd never seen her react to anything so strongly.

It was all I could do to assuage her distress. My attention returned to the TV set, and I began to feel her pain as I saw, coming down the stairs of a plane at La Guardia, Marilyn Monroe.

Or was it?

The woman was a carbon copy of Marilyn, wearing what looked to me like a platinum-blonde wig with big, dark sunglasses, although when I looked very closely, she appeared a bit taller. We stood in that living room with our mouths hanging open. We knew perfectly well that this was an impostor, but the viewing public sure didn't.

It was the first time, but hardly the last, that I saw Marilee break down. She held herself together for as long as she could, then she sobbed out loud, tears rolling down her cheeks. "Oh, my God! Even if I say nothing, I'm misquoted!"

Joe tried to comfort her. "Forget about it. There's nothing you can do," he told her.

Having faced so much of this publicity-grabbing attention himself, he knew that fighting it only drew more media attention along with the ensuing gossip.

Marilee couldn't believe how people could fabricate stories about her that way. When the papers ran the same story the next day, splashing it across the headlines, she was still distraught. I can imagine how difficult it was for her not to scream out to the whole world that the press was lying, but, brokenhearted as she was, she took Joe's advice and let it pass.

"What price fame?" she asked, and shook her head sadly. "Why do they call us stars, Junie? The stars are in the heavens. We're not stars; we're just working performers."

Marilee believed that to her core. I was constantly surprised at how naïve she seemed to be about her star status. I don't think she realized just how famous she was and how some people felt that it was important to be seen with her, or her facsimile. She honestly thought that she should be treated just like everyone else. She was such an honest person, and couldn't understand the lies that took their toll on her and would follow her even after her death.

10

WHAT PRICE FAME, INDEED

ONE STORY ABOUT MARILYN proves that the words *star* and *commodity* are interchangeable, just like the words *used* and *abused*.

We all know Marilyn Monroe for her beautiful blonde hair, but as her early photographs attest, she wasn't a natural blonde and her hair needed touching up periodically. Her real hair was limp and very thin. When she went before the cameras, she had additions, hairpieces like extensions, to make her hair appear fuller.

Once when she was visiting Mother she saw that her roots were getting a little dark, but she didn't want to go all the way back to Hollywood just to have her hair touched up. If she'd really wanted to, she could have had the world's best hair stylists flown in, but this was her time to visit with Mother for the intimate talks that only a mother, or surrogate mother, and daughter could have together.

Besides, Mother was a blonde, too—from the bottle, but blonde nonetheless. Being fairly knowledgeable about hair coloring, she offered to help, and Marilee was happy to let her. Times like this let Marilyn have the kind of talks she never had with her own mother.

Mother cared deeply about Marilyn and took the time to show it. Their talks weren't earth shattering, just conversations about life—and *real* life was what Marilyn longed for, since her life in Hollywood was synthetic at best. Paid lackeys fussed over her, but few, if any, dared tell her the truth.

This time, after Mother transformed her back into that sexy blonde once again, Marilyn said that she needed a haircut, too. Since

Mother was no expert in cutting hair, she phoned her favorite salon on Chestnut Street and off they went. When they walked into the salon, you can imagine the reaction: Jaws dropped. The staff was tongue-tied, but they scurried about and did a great job. Marilyn and Mother returned to the apartment to carry on with the rest of their day of good cooking and fun talk, as usual.

Not very glamorous, but that was how Marilyn enjoyed spending time with my mother every chance she got. She always made sure that her visits with Joe in San Francisco included some hours at my parents' apartment, where she felt happy and comfortable. I only wish she could have had more of them.

When I returned the next day from southern California, Marilyn wanted to do something she loved: walk the streets incognito and drink in the atmosphere. San Francisco was beautiful then, as it is today. The air temperature always stayed at a comfortable 60 or 70 degrees, perfect for a nice jaunt.

I think Marilyn felt more comfortable walking there than in Hollywood or Beverly Hills. Not that she wasn't recognizable everywhere she went, but her fans didn't expect to spot her in San Francisco. Besides, hiking up and down the steep hills was great for her thighs as well as being generally invigorating for the body and soothing for the spirit.

As usual, Marilee hadn't brought any comfortable clothes, so I loaned her a pair of my white ducks. She pulled on a long, curly, black wig that she'd brought home from the studio.

Earlier she'd explained to me that she had worn that terrible wig so she could visit a department store all by herself to buy Barbara Klein a necklace and earrings. Marilee sincerely appreciated Barbara's friendship and counseling and eagerly anticipated her reaction to the gift. Of course Barbara oohed and ahhed. I smiled, knowing that Barbara would probably never wear the jewelry, which to me looked gaudy.

Generous Marilyn shopped all by herself for this necklace to give to Barbara Klein.

At this gathering to celebrate DiMaggio's $250,000 skyroom, I'm wearing the necklace that Marilyn gave to Barbie. My Uncle Dominic shares an hors d'oeuvre with me.

Meanwhile, Mother was fed up seeing her in that oversized, out-of-style hairpiece, and took her shears to the curls in an effort to update it. It still looked ghastly, but Marilee didn't mind, and off we went.

We strolled down the streets of the City, talking and laughing and having a fine time until we came to the beauty salon where Mother had brought Marilyn the day before.

Marilee grabbed my hand.

"Junie," she gasped. "Look!"

We both fell silent, unable to believe what we were seeing. Hanging in the salon's front window were tiny packets of blonde snippets labeled MARILYN MONROE'S HAIR, priced at $100 apiece. We stood there for only a few moments, but a dark shadow descended over our day of fun, ruined by the reality that fame is measured in so many dollars and cents and that, to the general public, privacy meant nothing.

We didn't stop anywhere else, but immediately returned home to tell Mother what we had seen. Livid, she called my father at the restaurant and reported the incident in detail.

As I've mentioned, Father was very even-tempered and slow to anger, but this was one of the few times his Sicilian heritage reared its fiery head. I shouldn't have been surprised, since Father always championed those who were being injured or taken advantage of. Not stopping at home to calm down, he stormed out of DiMaggio's and went straight to the hair salon. Without a word and ignoring staff protests, he quietly gathered every packet of hair hanging in the window, and then, his face beet red, he shouted at the owner, "How dare you sell Marilyn's hair? Without her permission, no less?"

No one questioned my father, and when he needed it, he had a glare that could melt ice. He warned the shop owner never to take advantage of a celebrity again or she'd face severe legal consequences. Needless to say, the salon lost my mother as a customer, along with several of her friends.

That was just one example of what I saw over and again, how people think celebrities are little more than pricey commodities to be bought and sold, often without their permission. If you're an actress, fame and adoration come with the reality that you belong to a handful of powerful men holding your contract. You never ask questions. You say and do as you're told, or else. There are plenty of other hopefuls lined up in back of you, ready to do anything to achieve stardom at any cost. That's why that crazy world called Hollywood was not the place for me.

YOU ARE PROBABLY wondering why I call Marilyn "Marilee" sometimes. After she and I became friends, one day out of the blue, she told me to call her that. I couldn't imagine why, and looked at her quizzically.

"It's a combination of Marilyn and Lee," she said gleefully. To her it was a combination of her own name and my mother's. Her given name was Louise, but everyone knew her as Lee. Marilyn had grown so close to Mother, confiding in her like the mother she never had, that she wanted to honor her and use her name.

So Marilee she became, although no one else ever called her that. It wasn't Marilyn Monroe my family and I grew to love, but Marilee, with whom we laughed and even shed a few tears. It was our little friendship secret, albeit for just a few short years.

YOU NEVER SAW MARILYN wearing glasses in her movies, but she was so nearsighted that she could hardly see without them.

"I wear them only when I want to see," she'd tell us laughingly.

Her sunglasses were prescription lenses, too, so she could keep them on and maintain her image, but around my family she felt comfortable wearing her regular glasses because she knew we didn't care. We loved Marilee, not Marilyn Monroe the box-office star, but if someone she didn't know came into the room, off came the glasses and Marilyn from the screen came alive.

When it came to her public persona, she was a real trouper. Not many people knew that Marilyn got terrible headaches quite often. At least once a month they got extremely severe. Whenever we saw her grow pale, we knew she was in for a rough time. Her way was never to complain, even when the pain was excruciating.

Marilyn told me that during childbirth her mother went insane and that when she was very small, she was taken away from her mother for good. For me, who grew up in a big, caring family, it's hard to imagine what kind of impact that must have had on such a sensitive girl. And as I've said, Marilyn was always afraid that she would end up insane like her mother. She had no one to turn to; no one to ask the growing-up-female questions every young girl needs answers to. She told me of all the terrible experiences she had suffered going from foster home to foster home and how she just couldn't relate to any of them.

It must have been incredible for a sensitive Gemini, who can be so easily hurt, to try and adjust to the disregard and dislocations. When she was ten or eleven, she finally went to foster parents who were good. They had a daughter, too, and treated her like their own.

"They were the best," she said with a smile, the one time she smiled about those early years, which haunted her all the days of her life. The lessons from her years in foster care stayed with her. Early on, she had learned to never be a burden. If she wanted a family to let her stay with them, she didn't dare make waves.

MANY PEOPLE STILL imagine that Marilee was a dumb blonde. Her adoring multitudes also believed that all Marilyn thought about was sex, but that was true only of the characters she played.

Mother almost never repeated anything about what she and Marilyn talked about privately, but once when I was perhaps just a little envious, I remarked to my mother that Marilyn was so sexy and that I wished I could be more like her.

"Poor Marilyn hated sex," she blurted out. "Because she's a sex symbol they think she's in bed with everyone."

Once when she arrived, she looked sad and depressed. I didn't want to pry, but I knew somehow that it was one of those times when she'd felt forced to succumb to the advances of one of the degenerates who ran the studio. She knew that this type of sex was a career-maker or -breaker and that love was not the reason for sex in this land of plastic.

Marilyn told me that she wasn't even fond of sex with Joe, although she did love him. One time I asked her, "Did you ever have an orgasm?"

"What's that?" she answered. Marilyn felt an obligation to have sex with him as his wife, at least at the beginning, but through his patience and affection, I think she ultimately learned how to enjoy the beauties of lovemaking.

Marilyn did have standards and morals and held to them, but she had to survive in a business that didn't care a hoot for morals or feelings. She told me how the head honchos at 20th Century Fox chased her around the office, and she would give in to them quickly just to get it over with. She said that it hurt and that she hated it. I have to believe that Marilyn must have learned to turn off her emotions as a very young child. On the casting couch, believing that she had to sleep with wrinkled old men to survive in the business, she continued to turn them off. She protected herself by playing a part there, too. There were times, she told me, when she came home exhausted from a day's shoot, and some powerful old geezer telephoned. She said that just the sound of his voice made her skin crawl.

Filming "The Misfits"

All photographs courtesy of Doc Kaminski

Marilyn, taking notes for the next scene in "The Misfits." Perhaps she could have been more in charge of her own life had she lived longer.

Marilyn takes a break on the set, smiling as always.

Maybe one of her demons was taking temporary hold, but Marilyn tried to keep it together and do her best with Clark Gable and Montgomery Clift in "The Misfits."

Always in demand, Marilyn smiled and shared herself in so many ways. Although it was difficult to concentrate in the heat on location the Nevada sun never stopped her from spending a little time with everyone on the set.

Marilyn always took a moment to pose with people on the set.

There's no mistaking that Marilyn Monroe aura, even emerging from a swim.

On the set of "The Misfits," Marilyn takes a break from the desert heat to cool off.

Pigtails and towels. This was the real Marilyn coming to the surface on the set of "The Misfits." Most of the time she had to be the Marilyn the studio wanted her to be.

Fussed over on the set, Marilyn was really such a simple girl at heart.

Even dripping wet, Marilyn was a sight to see with those luscious lips and twinkling eyes.

Here's "little girl" Marilyn sharing a moment in a photo that photographer Doc Kaminski loved.

Three gals hangin' out on the set during a break in shooting "The Misfits." Even in pigtails, Marilyn glowed.

Marilyn, protecting that china-doll skin
from the strong desert sun.

Acting on horseback may have been a
challenge, but Marilyn was up to it.

Since Marilyn was always welcome in the home Barbara and I shared, we kept a terry cloth robe for Marilyn to lounge in after a shower, a clean tee-shirt, and a pair of jeans.

After some of the horrors of her studio sex, she would come to our place and stay in the shower for an hour or more. Obviously she wanted to wash away the terrible experience. Then she'd sit down to dinner and ask for second helpings. I think she wanted, consciously or not, to gain weight so that maybe they'd leave her alone. Food seemed to be her escape in other ways, too. At times she told us, "I don't care if I gain five pounds. I don't give a damn!"

Marilyn had many bouts of depression, and when she talked with us, the tears ran down her cheeks. It wasn't easy being a star, a possession of the studio and the public, but once she got out of that environment and rid herself of the cinematic war paint, she was just Marilee—a poor, lost soul who needed someone to talk with.

Marilyn told me that the one screen idol she identified with was Jean Harlow. I think she related to Harlow because she, too, had desperately tried to overcome the stereotype of being nothing more than a body on the screen. I believe that Marilyn hoped that she could avoid the tragedy that consumed Harlow.

There were several striking similarities in the two young stars' lives. Both Monroe and Harlow died young. Marilyn was thirty-six and Jean Harlow was just twenty-six. Jean Harlow was the first blonde bombshell. As a matter of fact, the term was coined for her. Both married in their teens, and while both actresses had on-screen energy and charisma that lit up audiences, neither had the chance to become the dramatic actress each believed she could be.

Jean's short life was the stuff that tabloids relish, and Marilyn's was no different. Jean died during the making of the movie *Saratoga* in 1937. The film was completed with a double, using long shots. The movie starred Clark Gable, who was quoted at the time as saying that he felt like he was acting with a "ghost."

Maybe that's a good description for both Jean Harlow and Marilyn Monroe. They flashed before our eyes for just an instant in time, yet today they're still worshipped as celluloid goddesses. It's also ironic that Marilyn's last movie, *The Misfits,* was with Clark Gable.

The man who was on the set to capture the moments of that final movie was Doc Kaminski. He was given exclusive rights to be on the set of the film in the Reno, Nevada, area for just over two months, shooting candid photographs behind the scenes. Doc Kaminski captured the Marilyn few knew, but the one who will live forever in his photos.

11

A SHELTERED LEGEND

I RECALL SOME PARTICULARLY touching moments during one of Marilyn's rare in-between times, when she wasn't making a movie and hadn't scheduled any personal appearances.

One day, script in hand, Marilyn came to visit Barbara and me in Beverly Hills. Often she brought a script with her to read and work on while she relaxed and got away from the rat race.

Sometimes I'd help by reading lines with her, but this was my day to watch TV cartoons. I loved to watch "The Wonderful World of Disney" show on ABC-TV, hosted by Walt himself. It debuted on October 27, 1954, and went on for several decades. This night "The Three Little Pigs" cartoon was on.

Disney presented wonderfully produced family programming, and for me the show was a must-see every week. I especially enjoyed watching cartoons, so I suggested to Marilyn that we watch together.

To my amazement, she said, "I've never watched a cartoon."

I thought that she was just teasing, so I teased her back.

"You must have never been a kid if you never saw a cartoon," I said. Then I realized that she was telling me the truth.

"As a girl I never got to do the ordinary things other kids did, like watching cartoons," she said, nearly crying.

I'm sure that she must have meant that she had never seen cartoons on television, but I almost believe that she never even went to the movies. What a life, or lack of one, for this sweet girl.

I felt terrible and apologized for kidding her about never having seen a cartoon. I wanted watching cartoons together to be a special experience for her, so I went into action.

"You're going to get the June DiMaggio cartoon-caper," I told her.

While she settled in on the sofa in front of the TV, I headed to the kitchen to make popcorn. I mean, what's a cartoon without popcorn, preferably homemade? I pulled out my biggest pan, poured in butter, sprinkled it with popcorn, and began to shake the pan vigorously over the medium open flame. No Jiffy Pop or microwave popcorn in those days. Toward the end, I lowered the flame so that the popcorn wouldn't get singed, then I added a touch of salt and voila! It was show time. Would you believe I still do it the old-fashioned way even today? Nothing tastes like freshly made popcorn, and the smell fills the whole house. That day my efforts were rewarded tenfold. I smiled to see this grown woman become a little girl before my very eyes, enjoying cartoons for perhaps for the first time.

Our Burmese cat, Minka, snuggled with Marilyn whenever she slept over on our roll-away bed. Yes, even at the peak of her fame, Marilyn Monroe slept on a simple roll-away bed in our home. Hardly the Ritz, but then again, what she coveted most was the simple things in life.

That night, as Marilee snuggled with Minka, I enjoyed watching her enthralled reactions more than I did the cartoon itself.

"Isn't that cute!" she blurted out. "Oh, that's darling! Isn't that adorable?"

Barbara came in the room, and as if on cue, Marilyn and I each took on the role of one of the little pigs. Barbara chuckled, threw up her hands, and left us to our entertainment.

After that delightful evening, it became our weekly ritual. Marilyn would come over for an early dinner whenever she could, and then it was popcorn with Uncle Walt. She loved it, and I loved having a partner in childlike glee.

SHE MAY HAVE ENJOYED cartoons, but let me be clear; Marilyn was no dimwit. Actually she was exceptionally bright. Her mind was inquisitive, quick and creative; to be a star of her magnitude took a lot of brains. Unfortunately, not enough people got to see that side of her. She loved to quote Ralph Waldo Emerson, for example. She didn't even need to look at the words on the page because she carried certain passages in her head and loved reciting them aloud. It was her way of sharing her emotions, and it left her feeling content. She loved the classics and she loved to learn, trying to take on life as quickly as she could. Perhaps she knew on a higher level that she'd have only a short time on earth to take it all in.

She knew I was raised by my Mormon grandmother, and she was curious to the point of wanting to explore more about my religion with me. At one time Marilyn expressed interest in possibly becoming a Mormon. Incidentally, Mormons don't drink, but for Marilyn that didn't present a problem, since she didn't care about smoking or drinking—even coffee or tea because they contained caffeine. I told her that there had to be more to changing one's religion than not drinking. It had to be a change of lifestyle and a commitment to the true beliefs of Mormonism. She took that to heart.

She was very spontaneous. She had to live on studio time for her endless rehearsals, performances, and appearances, so her time was limited, but Marilyn often took a chartered plane to fly north from Hollywood to see my parents in San Francisco. She flew chartered because commercial airlines eat up lots of passenger time in boarding and deplaning, and time was one commodity Marilyn rarely had in abundance.

She never really cared that much about clothes, at least not the glamorous type. When she finished shooting at the studio, sometimes she didn't even take time to change out of her costumes. She'd come directly from the sound stage to our Hollywood duplex still in costume and ask if she could wear my clothes, just as she did when she visited in San Francisco.

I vividly recall one particular time when she came in her pajamas with a mink coat wrapped over them.

"Junie," she said, "I didn't want to take the time to change."

This was not unusual for her. Many times she had such early morning calls that she'd arrive at the studio in the morning wearing her PJs. Why bother changing into clothes at three or four A.M. when she'd only have to change again into the clothes that wardrobe gave her for that day's scenes?

"No problem," I told her when she arrived. Although I was more bosomy than Marilyn—and I know that seems incredible—she could wear most of my clothes. I bristle when I read comments of those who look at Marilyn's bust line as if that were all that mattered about this superb lady. Back then, some women naturally had that sweater girl look. Marilyn was one and so was I. You may not believe this, but Marilyn said that she was envious of my size, a 42D. Of course, she said it in fun.

Periodically Mother took Marilyn shopping to get clothes she could leave at the apartment in San Francisco so that when she visited later she wouldn't have to bring anything with her. You'd be surprised at some of the places where she shopped. Around my family and me, she always felt comfortable being Norma Jeane and needed only knock-around clothes.

After Marilyn died, I was amazed to see a $10.95 pair of Levis that Mother bought for her at Sears & Roebuck sell at auction for thousands of dollars. What price fame, indeed?

WHEN SHE WAS WORKING, Marilyn had a grip on the reality of the business and took her acting seriously, but she also knew when she needed some time off. She had a great sense of fun, and when she played, she did it with gusto. Her life just didn't give her enough time for it.

Barbara taught her card games like canasta and gin rummy, and they played for a dime a game. Marilyn loved to play gin rummy with my mother, too, for the same stakes. She would come over with a few dimes, ready to go. Whenever she won she squealed, "Beat you, Lee!"

Mother also taught her how to play solitaire. Perhaps it was prophetic for her to learn that game, since she never seemed to have someone in her life long term.

There is a very lonely side to being a star. Once you reach the heights Marilyn did, few people allow you to come back down gently. They'd rather knock—or pull—you down. So I think part of Marilyn's enjoyment of playing games came from her love of being with us. She just wanted to be a regular person, part of a family—and she could count on us to treat her that way.

Marilyn could literally let her hair down around our family. She never wore her hideous black wig around us, only when she tried to venture out incognito. When visiting us, she braided her hair to get it out of the way, making her look like the sweetest little Dutch girl. Marilyn loved shopping with my mother, but that sometimes posed challenges because she didn't seem to realize how famous she was.

One time when Mother ran out of birdseed for Tommy, her pet cockatiel, and was headed out to Sears—a regular haunt of hers—to get more, Marilyn asked if she could go along. She thought that since it would be a quick stop, nobody would have the chance to recognize her, and so Marilyn didn't bother to wear any disguise.

Sure enough, when my mother had gone off to pay for the seeds at the pet department, a clerk recognized Marilyn in an instant. By the time Mother returned, a crowd had gathered, gushing, "Aren't you Marilyn Monroe?"

Marilyn never hesitated. Adopting a full Scandinavian accent, she went into a long bit about how she was just visiting the United States.

"Everyvun sinks I'm Marileen," she told them in a wacky sort of accent, "but my name is Eve Lindstrom."

When some of them still wanted her autograph, she went ahead and signed *Eve Lindstrom*.

On their way home Marilyn and Mother laughed so hard that they almost got sick.

MARILYN WAS SITTING in my mother's living room, gazing off into the distance overlooking the Marina as the clouds drifted slowly across the horizon. In her big blue eyes I saw a restless longing that reminded me of a pet shop kitten.

I also got the feeling that she was conjuring up something that was going to involve yours truly, and sure enough, she announced that she wanted to go for a walk.

Fall days in the Bay Area can be dull, gloomy, and chilly. By September the fog usually sets in and the sun doesn't show itself until late afternoon—if at all. This day was different, with an azure sky and puffy white clouds that my imagination could sculpt into any number of creatures.

Despite the beautiful weather, I wasn't in the mood for a walk, but Marilee had a way of convincing me to do things I didn't want to. To please her, I got dressed in my sweats to ward against the breeze coming in from the bay, and off we went.

Strolling along, we felt so alive. A walk along San Francisco's Marina green is always invigorating. Whether it's a foggy morning or a cool sunny afternoon, you feel raw ocean air from across the waves brushing your face, and it feels that all's well with the world. This day Alcatraz looked clear of fog, and the waves lapped gently on the shore. Marilyn was wearing her god-awful wig again.

We were both young and energetic, and we walked and conversed, laughing and gossiping like two teenagers. We talked about life and love, about our beaus and their good and bad points. She always confided her intimate thoughts with me, but I never pumped her for information.

Finally we were ready to plop down on one of the Marina benches. We split a pack of gum, and Marilee kept trying to pop the Juicy Fruit like bubble gum. I told her it was no use, although every once in a while she did manage to squeeze out a tiny bubble or two.

Suddenly dozens of pigeons descended around us, coming from all directions. Marilyn and I sat there for some time, watching them come and go.

She turned to me and said, "Awww, they want food, poor things."

They were used to being fed by passersby, but I realized that we had nothing to give them. The more we tried to shoo them away, the more they kept coming back, begging. Then Marilyn spit her wad of gum into her hand and held it out to the pigeons. One plucky bird quickly grabbed the morsel and tried to swallow it. He twisted and turned and shook his head furiously. At first we laughed, but the more that poor bird tried to free its beak, the more the gum stuck fast.

Marilyn realized that this little bird could asphyxiate or starve. She didn't intend to harm the poor pigeon; she was just impulsive. We realized we had to do something. The other pigeons scattered as we scurried after that one hapless bird, trying to snare him before he swallowed the gum and choked on it. It was as if that pigeon knew we were trying to help, because he didn't fly away. Thank heaven that our pursuit made him shake his head one last time and out flew the gum from his beak. *Then* he flew away.

We laughed so hard that we were desperate to get back to the apartment, and fast. Plus each of us wanted to be the first to tell the tale of the plucky pigeon. Marilyn won out, as usual, and her tale of the gummed-up pigeon gave Mother a good laugh. Of course, she chided us for giving chewing gum to an animal who can't chew. "I hope you've learned your lesson," she said.

Later, when Joe and my father arrived, Marilyn begged me to let her tell the story again of the Juicy Fruit that nearly took wing. I agreed, and Marilyn related every detail. Again.

12

OFF ON THE WRONG FOOT

As Marilee and Uncle Joe's wedding day drew closer, Marilee grew more and more excited. The big day was almost at hand, so she and Mother went shopping in search of the right outfit at I. Magnin's. They selected a gorgeous brown suit with brass buttons for her to wear. Marilyn was thrilled that it was a perfect fit, and assumed that she was ready to go.

"That suit is way too drab for a lovely woman like you," Mother said with aplomb, as if talking to her own daughter.

But now it was much too late to have it altered, so Mother took over. She went to her closet and tore through her wardrobe looking for something to jazz up the suit and make it star-worthy. She found exactly what she was looking for—a sophisticated satin evening suit that she loved. She removed its mink collar and decided to take off the sparkly rhinestone buttons as well. Carefully and lovingly, she sewed them on the new wedding suit by hand.

She even went back to I. Magnin's and, for about $20, bought Marilee a pair of rhinestone earrings to match. Mother wanted her to look her best for that special day, so she also bought a darling little hat adorned with feathers and rhinestones, which Marilyn kept for many years.

After her death, those same rhinestone earrings went on the auction block for thousands of dollars.

You can well appreciate why my father was his brother Joe's best man and my mother was Marilyn's matron of honor. She had, in essence, adopted Marilyn into her heart, and Marilyn in turn confided in her and counted on her. Mother never let her down, giving her all the advice and affection she could, and she never betrayed Marilee's confidence.

Joe and Marilyn were married on January 14, 1954, but a long married life was not meant to be. Joe was jealous in a variety of ways. He wanted not just a wife, but a typical Italian housewife. Once he married Marilyn, he expected her to give up her career—to him the perfectly natural, wifely thing to do. He had expected the same from his first wife.

But Marilyn had dreamed of a screen-acting career, worked diligently for it year after year, and had come too far toward that dream to end it all now. After all the sacrifices she had made to climb that ladder to stardom, how could she give it all up?

You'd think Uncle Joe would have learned a lesson or two from his first marriage to budding actress Dorothy Arnold. A youthful twenty-one years old when they met, Dorothy was already a contract starlet who appeared in many of Universal Studio's "B" pictures, as they were called, since they typically formed the second half of a double-feature.

When they married, Joe was at the apex of baseball fame. She was ambitious, too, and asked Joe to help her get a screen test so she could move up to better movie roles. With his connections, he got her a screen test at 20th Century Fox. Unfortunately, Dorothy spoke in a monotone with no inflection, which put her out of the running for a contract.

After her failure, Joe assumed that she would settle down and become the wife he always wanted and expected. To his Italian mind-set, that meant following him and his career, which at the time was blossoming. Dorothy wanted no part of Joe's "flunkies," as she called them. She had her own circle of friends, her own dreams and agenda for the future. Their only child, Joe Junior, was born on October 23, 1941, but their marriage lasted just two and a half years. Dorothy divorced Joe and took Joe Junior with her.

Another source of jealousy for Uncle Joe had to do with Marilyn and Joe's respective fame. He retired from baseball in 1951, when he was past his prime, while she was just reaching hers.

That February they had been married barely a month when she was asked to go on a four-day USO tour to entertain the troops in Korea.

And she went on the tour.

(Marilyn's generosity was ongoing, not a hit-or-miss thing. She brought home a hand-carved Chinese chess set as a special gift for Mother. A gorgeous golden vase that Mother displayed proudly was also a gift from Marilyn. They sit in my home to this day as a constant reminder to me how warm and generous Marilyn was. She shared the things she did because giving was something she needed to do for herself. It fulfilled something deep inside her. The gift's cost was irrelevant to her. It was the sentiment, the meaning behind the object, that counted. Money never meant that much to her.)

When she returned from the tour, I recall how she was on cloud nine after all the applause she'd received from the young men, but when she began sharing her experiences, Joe grew annoyed. Instead of letting her bask in her moment in the sun, he felt driven to tell her how much applause *he'd* received in *his* glory days, when *he* went overseas.

Their clash of egos intensified and was to grow even stronger.

Still, they were very much in love.

Joe absolutely adored Marilyn, the only real love of his life, but their marriage was doomed to fail. Marilyn was a major star going from movie to movie with a packed schedule. Although she loved being domestic, it was more of a hobby for her at the time. Joe, on the other hand, wanted a full-time, Italian-style homebody who would go grocery shopping and be there with dinner waiting every night when he came home.

Arm in arm, my mother, Lee, was Marlyn's
matron-of-honor when she married
Uncle Joe at City Hall on January 14,
1954. My father, Tom, who was Uncle Joe's
best man, walks just behind my mother.

Marilyn and Joe enjoy a special moment
after their wedding, while my mother,
Lee, and the wife of Joe's good friend
Reno Barsocchini look on.

A handwriten note from Marilyn to my mother and father, thanking them for all their love and support.

Dear Lee and Tom,

    We were so happy to receive your lovely gift.

    We also thank you for all the moral support we received from you both January 14th.

              Love,

              Marilyn

Because Joe wanted and loved her so much, he simply couldn't see her for what she was—a star that the public idolized. She was far beyond the little domestic partner Joe was seeking, and I couldn't imagine her being a part of that scenario for any length of time.

Acclaim from her overseas tour only served to exacerbate Joe's resentment. Add to that his jealousy of her sexy work on screen, and I could see trouble brewing.

When Marilyn made movies, she obviously had to perform love scenes with male stars. That was expected of any attractive young female lead, as it is today, but Joe had an "I own you" attitude that so many Italian men of his generation took with their wives. Marilyn's on-screen lovemaking made him see red.

WHILE MARILYN AND JOE struggled with their hopes and expectations about one another, my life went on at a hectic pace. Partying with songwriter Hoagland "Hoagy" Howard Carmichael, for instance, was like being in a whirlwind. He gave us sensational songs, including "Stardust," "Georgia on My Mind," "Up the Lazy River," and many more romantic and memorable tunes.

I came to know Hoagy because his sister, Georgia Maxwell, and Barbara Klein were co-practitioners in metaphysics. Hoagy lived with his sisters and mother off Sunset Boulevard in Hollywood.

He had heard me sing, but I didn't meet him until he came to a party at my home with his sister. Many times he sat at the grand piano in Barbara's den, writing songs for hours on end. He wrote "Junie's Song" just for me. Hoagy could coax a song out of a piano that would tug at your heartstrings.

I would go to see Hoagy's mother, Lida—Mommy Carmichael, we called her—to bring strawberries she loved from the farmer's market.

Hoagy always told me how glad he was that his mother had me to care about her. She had been a fabulous ragtime pianist, and I loved to hear her play.

Hoagy was very generous to me, although I noticed that his generosity did not extend to his two sons. After one of my performances, he presented me with a special gift: a gold lipstick compact with piano keys on the top that today still plays "Stardust" when you open it.

However, when it came to business, he really didn't help anyone. Since he and Barbara were good friends, she once asked if he might put in a good word to help me land a role. In no uncertain terms, he told Barbara that he never asked friends for help, or gave any. On the other hand, when it came to helping his sisters, Hoagy was a totally different person. For example, when Georgia's husband deserted her, Hoagy hired her to do his bookkeeping.

Unfortunately, he couldn't do much to help his younger sister, although he tried. After falling in love with a married man, she became an alcoholic. Her life spiraled out of control and she died young.

When his dear mother died, I was there to help him, as he asked me to be. We dressed his mother elegantly. He wanted her to look lovely even at the last. While waiting for the undertaker to come, Hoagy sat at the piano and began playing a piece I had never heard before or since.

He explained that he had written "May Time" for his mom and wanted to play it for her one last time. Georgia arrived a short time later, but Hoagy kept on playing. He had written a whole symphony in his mother's honor, and he played it that day from beginning to end as a final tribute.

That night Hoagy and Georgia came to my house. During dinner we reminisced about all the good times we'd had with their mother and cried a little as Hoagy discussed arrangements to lay her to rest. To this day I'm puzzled as to how Hoagy could be so cold to his own children's needs, yet so loving to his sisters and mother.

HOAGY WAS ALSO into ESP, and he often called to ask me to tell him my perceptions.

To this day I receive perceptions about people, usually at three in the morning or three in the afternoon. They don't happen every day, but when they do I break into a cold sweat. I've appeared on stage with Harold Sherman, the ESP guru of the day, to talk about extrasensory perceptions.

My ability was both a blessing and a curse for me. I always told Hoagy that impressions came to me when they came: I couldn't force myself to feel things, and I refused to make anything up.

He wasn't too happy with that answer, but I had to be true to what God gave me. I made no profit from it and used my gift only to help people, but there were several times when I did have a perception for Hoagy.

BECAUSE OF MY WORK in film and television, I was invited many places. Hoagy and I always went to quite a few parties together, but we loved to separate, mingle, and meet lots of different people.

Peggy Lee was one of the great Big Band singers and recording artists of her time. A dynamo of energy, she threw great bashes with all the trimmings and spared no expense. Stars would perform for one another, food and drink flowed, and the night became one big festival of music, revelry, and mutual appreciation.

At one of her A-list shindigs, Peggy came to me and said that she thought I was a good singer and actress.

"You have such a big voice and a perfect technique," she told me.

Since I was just getting established in the business, it was quite a compliment for me to hear this from a singer with such a stellar reputation, but the conversation wasn't over.

"I want to talk with you about something privately," Peggy whispered.

That seemed a little quirky, but I assumed it was the way Hollywood types behaved, and my curiosity was piqued. She ushered me out of the throng of partygoers to her bedroom. I was somewhat wary, but so far it was all innocent.

I may have been tiny in stature, but not in willpower. We sat on the settee at the foot of her bed, and I couldn't hold it in any longer. My voice rising to a brassy tone, I said, "What are we doing here?"

With drink in hand—not unusual for her—Peggy looked at me with those lovely, romantic eyes of hers. I was just about to bolt when she got right to the point.

"I want you to look at something," she said, indicating a tiny black-and-white television monitor on which then appeared a screen test.

"Give me your opinion of the acting," she said calmly.

That took the air out of my suspicions. I was flattered that she cared what I thought, so I sat silently, intently watching the tiny screen before me.

The starring actor was Dewey Martin, Peggy's husband at the time—her third, if my count is right. When the screen went blank, Peggy looked me squarely in the eye and asked, "What do you think of him?"

For a moment I hesitated, but I had the impression that she didn't want me to mince words.

"He stinks," I said, figuring that she already knew as much and just needed confirmation.

"You hit the nail on the head," Peggy agreed. "I know he's a terrible actor, but I wanted another opinion, since I'm married to him."

It seemed that in order to film a TV pilot Dewey wanted his new wife to invest $100,000. In those days those were very big bucks for a TV show. I told her honestly that she'd be crazy to throw her money away, but after all, he was her husband, and it was her decision.

We chatted a while longer, then went back downstairs to rejoin the crowd. I sang, as I usually did at parties like this, as if nothing had happened, but I was privately curious what Peggy would do.

The ending to this story is short, but not so sweet: Peggy told Dewey that she would not bankroll his venture, and that was the end of that TV show.

13

FROM HOWARD HUGHES TO
THE SEVEN YEAR ITCH

AT THE TIME, Barbara Klein was conducting motivational classes for the Church of Religious Science, where show business people came seeking self-understanding. Many stars, including Peggy Lee, flocked to Barbara's lectures.

They soon became fast friends, and Peggy became a frequent guest at Barbara's and my apartment. Barbara talked with Peggy as a practitioner of metaphysics and helped coach her about how to best use her voice.

One evening I asked Peggy to dinner. She so loved the frittatas I prepared that she took home the leftovers and asked, "When are you planning to make them again?" Long years later, when I spoke with Peggy after Barbara's death in September 1998, she still remembered how my frittatas had titillated her taste buds.

THEN THERE WAS Howard Hughes: a man part genius, part recluse, and perhaps part madman. Long before he adopted his long nails, long hair, and sanitized, reclusive ways, the younger Howard Hughes achieved a major success—or debacle, depending on how you view it—for actress Jane Russell with the movie *The Outlaw*.

Hughes had made a nationwide search for the star of the film before casting her. He even had his engineers design a special cantilevered bra to enhance the appearance of Jane's bust, although it was never used in the picture. But the movie defied the stringent censorship guidelines then set up through something called the Hayes Code.

The Hayes Code, "a code to govern the making of talking, synchronized and silent motion pictures," was formally adopted by The Association of Motion Picture Producers, Inc., and the Motion Picture Producers and Distributors of America, Inc., in March 1930. In general, the code purported to safeguard "wholesome entertainment."

The Outlaw was supposed to come out in 1941, but some changes had to be made, so it was released in 1943.

Talent didn't make a star in Howard Hughes' mind: breast size did.

I had an encounter with this multitalented mogul in 1954, when I auditioned for a movie role to portray an Indian girl. Five hundred girls auditioned for the part. Five were chosen, and I made the cut—after all, I did wear a D-cup brassiere. I honestly think that Hughes was trying to create another Jane Russell—and it didn't hurt that I was a competent actress.

The five of us who were chosen were given screen tests, and—surprise, surprise!—I won out to star in the movie. I was excited. After all, this could be a major break for me, perhaps even a first step to stardom. My agent, Earl Kramer, uncle of producer Stanley Kramer, was drooling over the nice little 10 percent he would get from my potential contract. Off we drove to meet Hughes and his accountant at Lucy's Restaurant. I'd like to think my agent didn't know what was to come, but if he did, he didn't warn me.

It was late in the afternoon. I sat nervously waiting for the meeting to begin. Finally Hughes and his accountant arrived, and was I shocked. In walked this scruffy, unkempt man wearing dirty white trousers and filthy sneakers. I imagine this was a precursor to his odd behavior and appearance later in life. Without much in the way of greeting, Hughes asked me what I wanted to eat and got right down to specifics.

Before I could give my order, he said, "I'm gonna make a big star out of you."

I guess he expected me to swoon, but I was starved, and first I wanted to eat.

"I'll set you up with your own apartment at the Sunset Towers," he went on. "I want you to be available to me when I call. You'll have no other boyfriends."

What he was saying is that he would own me, and he said it as if he was ordering off the menu and I was the appetizer, entrée, and dessert.

But he wasn't finished.

"I'll give you $100,000 before the film begins, and a lucrative seven-year contract," he said. "What do you say to that?"

My agent's eyes had dollar signs in them. He was in heaven, thinking I'd bought the deal hook, line, and sinker. I knew what my answer was going to be, but I decided that at least I'd get a good meal out of it first. "What's for lunch?" I said brightly.

I ordered the most expensive item on the menu, guinea hen with all the trimmings. I ate ravenously, but Hughes was patient. When I finally looked up from my plate, he asked, "So what do you think?"

I sat up as tall as I could.

"Mr. Hughes," I said, "I already have a wonderful roommate by the name of Barbara Klein at 421 North Doheny Drive, so I don't need your apartment at the Sunset Towers. I already have a boyfriend whom I adore, so I'll pass on your on-call offer. That's my final answer."

I never gave him a moment to interrupt. I wanted to finish what I had to say before I lost my nerve.

"I do not now, nor will I ever, have the desire to have sex with you," I continued, "and there's no way I'm signing a seven-year contract. If I do, I'm trapped. I know what you did with Jane Russell, and I am nobody's property to do with as you wish, but thank you very much for the lovely lunch."

That day Mr. Hughes might have learned that not every woman would jump at the snap of his fingers. I was very independent and knew what I wanted. It certainly wasn't to join Howard Hughes in bed, no matter how powerful he was or what prize he dangled in front of me. That was the end of that meeting. Neither he nor my agent was pleased, but I had a great lunch.

IN 1954, AFTER Marilyn completed *The Seven Year Itch*, the movie she remains famous for even today, Joe started to lose his cool. I could see that it was not a good portent for him to be flying off the handle such a short time after he and Marilyn were married. The flare-up arose over one of her last scenes in *The Seven Year Itch*, the legendary one where she stands atop a New York subway grate at Lexington Avenue and 52nd and the whoosh of air from a passing train below sends her dress flying up in a provocative way.

The scene had to be shot over and over, and Joe was there the whole time, watching off-camera. Every time Marilyn's dress flew up, the crowd cheered hysterically. It seemed that her panties were a bit on the sheer side. A second pair was called for, shooting resumed, and still the crowd went wild each time the dress lifted to reveal Marilyn's skivvies.

In the movie business, slip-ups and embarrassments are part of movie making, but Joe was no actor, and he was not amused. Although what that crowd saw was nothing by today's standards, he believed that his wife was all his and that no one but him should see what those folks saw, again and again, that day.

For some reason, none of that New York footage ever made it to the final cut. The scene was filmed again on a California sound stage, on a set exactly duplicating the street and buildings of New York. Later, when a cutout of the famous pose traveled the movie circuit and loomed over skylines around the country, Joe fumed all over again.

He didn't realize that Marilyn already belonged to the people she entertained from the big screen. Her fans were dedicated to her image, regardless of who the real Marilyn might be. Joe, ready to retire and settle down, and Marilyn, still reaching for the stars, were just not on the same page. It didn't help that Joe was the silent type, while Marilyn loved a rousing discussion. Also, I have to admit that Joe had a temper. When playing baseball, he would get furious at any umpire who made what he thought was a bad call—but Joe wasn't violent, regardless of what you may have read. Marilyn never once said that Joe lifted a hand to her, and I believe that if he had, she would have said something to Mother or me.

What Marilyn did say was that he gave her the silent treatment. That was a DiMaggio weapon, and Joe once used it on Marilyn for three months. Clamming up and saying nothing can be worse than most shouting. I think that Joe's inability to speak about his feelings and his use of silence to punish Marilyn were the straws that broke the camel's back.

Marilyn hated being ignored, and she couldn't understand why Joe treated her as he did. She needed people who cared about *her*, not her star status. Throughout her young years, she never had the tender closeness that she later received from the DiMaggio family, but Joe's silent treatment was sheer torture for her.

Marilyn came to my mother for advice. Mother, of course, would never stand for the kind of nonsense Joe was capable of. She told Marilyn that my father had given her the silent treatment just one time, and she said to him, "If you do that one more time, I'll pack your bags myself." And she meant it.

I, on the other hand, couldn't respond the same way. Father gave me the silent treatment once, too. I guess it was a common trait of the DiMaggio brothers. I had made a mistake without even knowing it. When my agent—also a good friend—and I were in San Francisco, I took him to DiMaggio's for dinner. When it came time to say goodbye to my parents, Father wouldn't speak to me. I couldn't understand why, and he wasn't about to tell me. I didn't have time to explore the situation because I had to get back to southern California for work.

His silence went on for six months. Every time I called home and Father answered, he would say nothing and hand the phone to my mother. He wouldn't even tell her why he was giving me the silent treatment, so we were both baffled.

The next time I was in the Bay Area, I cornered Father, and this time I was insistent.

"Why are you giving me the silent treatment?" I asked. "I'm very confused. What did I do?"

I guess Father felt that I'd been punished enough, and he lashed out at me.

"How dare you bring that agent with you to DiMaggio's for dinner?" he shouted. "He's a married man!"

At first I was shocked, then I began to laugh. "Of course," I explained. "I know he's married. He's not my lover, he's my agent, and a good friend who just happens to be married."

Presto! That's all it took, and we were back on speaking terms. So you can see why Mother wasn't about to let Joe get away with that same nonsense. She told Marilyn never to take that kind of treatment from anyone, no matter how much she loved him. Marilyn took

Mother's advice to heart. She filed for divorce. It was the silence, not any physical abuse, that Marilyn couldn't endure.

❧

WHILE THIS WAS GOING ON, Hoagy Carmichael and I made the rounds at a variety of private functions. Another reason he liked having me around was because as a Mormon I never touched alcohol. He, however, was known to kick back a few—quite a few. And if he didn't like what was being served, he brought his own booze, Pinch Bottle Scotch.

Hoagy owned one of the first Italian sports cars ever made, which to me was just his ferry home. Nowadays you'd call me his designated driver, but Hoagy was charming and funny, a good friend, and I loved his company, although ours was definitely not a love affair—at least not on my end.

For fifteen years Hoagy had been dating a lady he called Quacky, who absolutely adored him. Her real name was Dorothy Wanda McKay. Hoagy, rogue that he was, kept putting her off. Once he asked her to come and hear me sing, telling her, "I want you to see the girl I want to marry."

I was performing for a *Variety* magazine event at a prominent hotel in Hollywood. After the performance, Quacky came backstage alone.

"Hoagy is very fond of you," she began.

"I know," I replied, "but you have nothing to worry about. I would never make it with Hoagy. I already have a boyfriend."

Just as I uttered those words, my boyfriend Earl Colbert arrived. A strapping six-foot-two, he was a jazz guitarist touring with the Martha Raye Show. Martha, the well-known comedienne, was nicknamed "The Big Mouth."

Hoagy Carmichael adored me, but to me he was a great songwriter and friend.

Of course songwriter Hoagy Carmichael would give me a gift with a piano on it, but guess what? When you open this lovely compact, it plays "Stardust."

Hoagy was a real character, but he was always very supportive of me and interested in my ESP abilities.

Palm Springs
A Sunny Monday

Dear Junie,

Just wanted to tell you that I understand your note very well and destroyed same.

Also want to wish you happiness where you are. Please wish your mother my best and you just do as you damn please. And take no guff because you are a very special type of person.

Let me know the latest ESP deal. Very interesting.

Much love,
Hoagy

I'm back and forth — P. Springs and L.A.

I explained to Quacky why I went to parties with Hoagy and said that we'd always be just friends, nothing more. You'd think that episode would end his drive to marry me, but no; not that Hoagy Carmichael and I were ever intimate, we were just good friends, almost like family. At least that's how I felt. He, on the other hand, was very much in love with me.

One Christmas my mother came to visit in Beverly Hills. Hoagy invited her to lunch, apparently with an ulterior motive in mind. I was invited, too, so Mother and I arrived at his penthouse on Sunset Boulevard, just two blocks from Scandia's Family Restaurant. I suspected that he might want to get on her good side, but I got more than I bargained for. Then again, so did Hoagy.

As always, Mother took things in stride. She settled down, lit a cigarette, took off her shoes, and made herself at home. Hoagy proudly announced that he was the new spokesman for a canned food company. He went to his kitchenette, opened a can of their beef stew, scooped it into a bowl, and set it down in front of her.

Remember, my mother was a gourmet chef and restaurateur, proud to serve only the finest foods. She took one glance at the stew, looked at Hoagy, and asked him, "Is this out of a can?"

"Yes," Hoagy said, "but it's delicious."

Mother took one bite and looked up once again.

"Do you like this stuff?" she asked.

He nodded.

"You eat it, then," she said. "I wouldn't feed this to my dog. Just give me a cocktail instead."

Never missing a beat, Hoagy admitted that he had another reason for this invitation.

"I want to ask for your daughter's hand in marriage," he blurted out, "but she told me she can't marry a man older than her father."

My jaw almost hit the floor. Here again, Hoagy was taking matters into his own hands, and without my permission.

Mother drew a long drag on her cigarette, as she often did when she was getting ready to let someone have it. The moment of truth! She looked him straight in the eye.

"Well," she said. "You are older. You've got gray hair. Just how old are you?"

"Never mind," Hoagy replied.

And that was the end of that.

"I'll have that drink now," said Mother.

"I'll make mine a double," Hoagy said.

You'd think that would have finally put an end to his pursuit, but it didn't. I was at my cabin in northern California when he called me and offered to deposit a million dollars in the bank in my name if I would marry him.

By then I had had enough and said, "Hoagy, I don't need your money, and I won't take it. Even if I were broke, I wouldn't marry you, and no amount of money would get me to say yes."

To my way of thinking, money doesn't buy happiness. I saw too many stars with great wealth, and they were still very unhappy.

I did like Hoagy a lot, but to me he was just a short little guy with a tough exterior, while my boyfriends were always very refined and extremely tall.

"Why don't you marry Quacky?" I asked him. "She loves you so much."

Years later, in 1977, he finally did, and I was very happy for them. They stayed together until he passed on in 1981. Meanwhile, I'm glad I could call him a friend.

14

MARILEE ALONE AGAIN

UNCLE JOE AND MARILYN'S divorce became final on October 17, 1954. They were married for 286 days. Perhaps at another time and in another place it would have worked. It wasn't that their love for each other ended; it was just sidetracked.

Joe so regretted what he had done to cause his breakup with Marilyn, and he rued his actions for the rest of his life. He never fell out of love with her. I know that it just took him a while to come to his senses and realize that his Italian pride got in the way, and what he had done was wrong. His big mistake was trying to change a star into a wife.

For her part, Marilyn considered him the protector she could always count on, and Joe did a good job of looking out for her. It didn't matter to him that they weren't together; in his mind and heart they were never totally apart.

AFTER MARILYN DIVORCED Joe, I didn't see her quite as much, but we remained friends even after her marriage to Arthur Miller. By this time, regardless of her relationship with my Uncle Joe, she had become a member of the family. She enjoyed visiting Barbara and me for a number of reasons: friendship, good conversation, understanding, intimate counseling from Barbara and, of course, the great food I always prepared for her.

She needed true friends who didn't demand anything of her. We never would accept money or large gifts from her, but I do remember one time when Barbara accepted a lovely token.

Marilyn lived just a short distance away from our place in Beverly Hills and often came over unannounced, usually without makeup. If she came directly from the studio, the first thing she did was wash it all off. The sun was shining this day when a smiling Marilyn came bounding over, wearing a long blue chiffon scarf that flowed delicately over her shoulders. It was identical to the scarves she'd worn for the dance number in *Bus Stop,* and throughout the movie.

"For you, darling," she told Barbara, handing her the scarf.

"They'll never miss it," she said.

The delicate blue scarf Marilyn wore right off the set and gave to Barbara Klein after one of their counseling sessions. She truly admired Barbie.

Her purpose in coming directly from the set was to put this treasure directly into Barbara's hands. Barbara kept that scarf until the day she died.

I didn't want to see the auctioneer's hammer flatten one of the last mementos of our Marilee into a dollars-and-cents item, so after Barbara died, I gave it as a birthday present to a special friend who's an avid fan and a dedicated collector of Marilyn Monroe memorabilia. I know she will treasure that scarf forever, too.

Marilee never ever did anything halfway. She dearly loved my mother's Italian rum cake, a treasure made from scratch. Marilyn had sampled the cake more than a few times at my parents' apartment and was hooked on this tasty pastry. Mother's cake was tremendously rich, but that's exactly the way Marilyn loved it.

One day she was talking to my mother in San Francisco from Hollywood. Mother was explaining how to make the cake, which she was baking at the time, and how completing the process takes the better part of a day. They talked for quite a while before Marilyn said abruptly that she had to run. Knowing that she was always busy, Mother said good-bye and went on baking her rum cake.

I guess that Marilyn must have really wanted a taste of that cake.

Just a few hours later there was a knock at the door. To my mother's amazement there stood Marilyn, out of breath from bounding up two flights of stairs. Believe it or not, she had flown to San Francisco just for a taste of my mother's rum cake.

IT WASN'T UNUSUAL to run into celebrities at my parents' apartment, but one day in 1955 I walked into their living room and came face to face with the one and only Ethel Merman, sitting at our dining room table enjoying Mother's lasagna.

This lady with a voice bigger than she was had already become legendary on stage and screen, but at first I didn't recognize her. She wasn't wearing stage makeup, and her trademark big hair was pulled back in a bun. Even though I knew better, I supposed—like the rest of her fans—that from dawn to dusk she looked just like she did on stage.

How did she come to have dinner at my parents'? A family member was involved in a film Ethel was shooting in San Francisco and brought her to DiMaggio's Restaurant for dinner on a night when Uncle Joe happened to be there. They started talking, and Joe told her he was going to my mother's place for homemade lasagna.

When Ethel remarked how much she loved lasagna, Joe quickly invited her along. That was the DiMaggio way, and Ethel didn't hesitate to accept the invitation.

When I finally realized who was sitting at my mother's table, I gushed over her. I couldn't resist asking if she would sing, "There's No Business Like Show Business," her signature song.

Never missing a beat, she stood up from the table and said, "I'm not used to singing sitting down."

When she started to sing, there was no mistaking that this was the real McCoy. What a voice she had—and she sure didn't need a microphone. Her voice resonated across the room as it did on every stage where she performed.

It was a glorious evening with great conversation and getting to know the real personality behind that one-of-a kind voice. Ethel was quite down to earth and shared some of her show business experiences. Mother proudly told her that I was a singer, too, and Ethel asked me to sing for her.

I stood up tall and with all my might delivered my own signature song, "One Night of Love." Even Uncle Joe was surprised. He said laughingly, "Your voice is as big as Ethel's."

She put her arms around me and cooed in that husky voice of hers, "You have a great voice, darling," and kissed me on the cheek. They don't make them that way anymore; she was a one-of-a-kind star and a real lady.

It was in the early '50s, too, that I met Hungarian-born Baron Sepy Dubronyi at the Cuban Art Center in Los Angeles. Long before the Castro era he was selling Cuban art, and, yes, he was a real-life baron with a coat of arms to go with it. I can truly say he was incredible in the arts of love and life.

I still have some of the statues he gave me. The baron wanted me to travel with him at a time when I was still into my career. During the time he was in Hollywood, we saw a lot of each other. From him I learned to go after what I want in life, always keeping in mind three very important lessons:

Lesson #1: *You never get anything in life without paying for it.*

Lesson # 2: *Always use all your personality and emotions.*

Lesson #3: *Never depend on someone else to do things for you.*

And he showed me that those lessons were true.

One evening he called and suggested that we go to Earl Carroll's, the best-known celebrity club of its time. Anyone who was anyone in Los Angeles, from stars and agents to directors and producers, had to be seen there. I wondered if we could get in without having made reservations months in advance.

"Not to worry," Sepy told me.

We pulled up to valet parking in his huge Chrysler with the royal Hungarian crest on it, got out, and marched right in. Naturally, the maître d' told Sepy what he told everyone; that he had no tables. Sepy slipped him fifty dollars, a great deal of money in those days, and turned to me.

"Cuckoo," he said softly, "Money speaks loudly."

He thought his pet name for me was cute. I hated it, but we not only got a table, we got one in the front. The entertainers could practically sit on our laps. That was when I learned Lesson #1: *You never get anything in life without paying for it.*

One day we had just finished a set of tennis at the home of Hal Roach, the producer of the popular "Our Gang" series. At the time, Barbara Klein was teaching his kids how to swim, and Hal's wife insisted that Sepy and I use their tennis courts whenever we wanted.

Sepy, truly a huckster who was ready to cut a deal at any time, always kept his first-class collection of Cuban costume jewelry in his Chrysler. One day he asked me the names of some stars in Hollywood he could meet so that he could show them his line.

I mentioned a few names, and when I came to Joan Crawford's he saw dollar signs.

"Let's go see her," he said.

I was shocked. You didn't just show up unannounced at Joan Crawford's home, especially not in your tennis clothes, but we did. How he got her address, I'll never know. We pulled up in front of her house and he knocked at the door. When the butler answered, Sepy quickly handed him his card and asked to see Miss Crawford.

My jaw dropped when Joan Crawford came to the door. Sepy took her hand and kissed it in his suave, continental way. In his other hand he held his most stunning piece of jewelry set with an extraordinary stone—huge and very impressive.

"As beautiful as you are, this stone belongs on your finger," he said, slipping it on. "Would you like to see the rest of the collection?"

Miss Crawford showed us to her lanai. I said nothing as Sepy explained how he came to amass his collection, and asked her, "Might I interest you in any additional pieces?"

She told him she was interested, indeed.

"So many times, I go out shopping or in public, and I don't want to wear my real jewelry," she said.

She praised the beauty of his selections and how authentic his stones appeared.

"They could easily substitute for the genuine article," she said, admiring them.

She bought the whole collection he had with him, all $7,500 of it. With me standing there, still in shock, he kissed her hand once more and said, "I do hope you will enjoy wearing every one of them."

Then the Baron whisked me—stunned and impressed—away. That was when Lesson #2 popped into my head: *You must always use your personality and emotion.*

Sepy used them, abused them, and carried them to new heights. He combined the suave manners of royalty with the tenacity of a street-smart kid.

Another time, while window shopping in Los Angeles, Sepy and I passed by a display in I. Magnin. He stopped to study it and declared, "Their windows will be so much more attractive when they display my Cuban art along with the clothes."

Once again he had no appointment. He knew no one at the store, and neither did I, but that had never stopped Sepy. He marched right in to find two young men decorating one of the windows. Not wanting to waste time with hired help, Sepy asked for their boss. Too surprised to think twice, the young decorators told us the name and off we went to the main office.

Everyone was so startled by Sepy's bold manner that they let him pass. When he made it to the head office and the big guy asked who the heck he was, Sepy stood up straight and tall to introduce himself.

"I am Baron Sepy Dubronyi, come to add life to your windows," he said, explaining about his art and how it would enhance the clothing display. Before I knew it, he had the go-ahead to do so.

He walked back to the two designers and went straight to work on the windows, positioning the art objects (also stowed in the Chrysler at all times) among the fashions.   Every single piece of his art sold. The Baron had done it again, and Lesson #3 came to my mind: *Never depend on someone else.*

Sepy asked me to return with him to Cuba to star in a new club he had just opened. In those days, Havana was like present-day Las Vegas. He knew how deeply I felt about Barbara Klein, who had helped me so much with my career, and invited her to come with us. What he didn't realize was that a number of stars depended on Barbara as their vocal coach, and her leaving them would be quite impossible.

Moreover, my career was taking off quite nicely. I was rehearsing for a part in the Dean Martin movie *Ten Thousand Bedrooms*, and I wasn't about to give up a chance like that. I told Sepy "no."

The Baron was not to be deterred. Without my permission or even alerting me, he made the trek to San Francisco to ask my parents for my hand in marriage. To sweeten the offer, he brought Mother a huge box of candy, but he hadn't counted on my parents' wry sense of humor. Mother passed him off to Father, who foisted him back on Mother. Back and forth; they had him going like a ping-pong ball.

Finally, mercifully, they told him that it was really my decision.

"June is the one who has to sleep with you and cook for you," Mother said. "It's her choice, not ours, who she will marry."

The Baron took the hint and left. I never saw him again, but I had learned his three lessons, stored them away, and definitely used them.

15

NAÏVETÉ PERSONIFIED

As a woman, I'd grown pretty experienced by now, but as a performer I remained very naïve. Even though I'd been in many shows and knew of the experiences actresses had with their leading men in those days, I still believed that if I just worked hard, my talent would win out and I could be a star.

After a brief encounter with Ida Lupino, my eyes were opened very wide, indeed. She wanted to direct a movie musical about a ballet dancer. I auditioned, and I was in. I wouldn't have to dance, but it was a starring role nevertheless. She even added a song for me to sing that wasn't in the original script. My agent was ecstatic about my starring in this movie, but those were dollar signs in his eyes, not a marquee billing.

When I met Ida in the agent's office, she seemed nice enough. "Can you come to our house to read the script?" she asked me. "We can work on it together."

She was married to producer Howard Duff at the time, and since he was producing this movie, she wanted me to meet him.

When I got to their house, Howard Duff was nowhere to be seen. I thought he must have been called away. Then Ida sat next to me and said we should run through the love scenes so that we could "get comfortable" with them. Okay, I thought to myself, I could accept that. I was ready to throw myself into the scene when she laid a juicy one on my lips and tried to kiss me more.

147

None of this touchy-feely stuff with other females for me—good movie or bad! I had many loves in my life, but they all had deep, resonant voices—and the right parts in the right places.

Ida continued to follow me around her living room for several minutes. Finally I grabbed my coat, swung around the couch for one more lap, and dashed out the door. I fled into the street and made a bee-line back to the safety of my own home.

The next day I went crying to my agent's office and asked if he knew she was a lesbian or possibly a bisexual. He knew exactly what had gone on, but he wanted his 10 percent cut of my salary. Besides, most starlets at that time would do anything to get a good part.

Not me.

I told him absolutely not, and so another Hollywood credit became only a might-have-been. Other episodes like this began to pile up, and you can see why I made the decisions I did to get out of this life far earlier than most other actresses.

❦

I REALLY WASN'T THE party-girl type, and at some shindigs I was the only one who hadn't had even a single sip of booze. Because I had my head on straight, people shared their secrets, and I would hear—and remember—all kinds of gossip.

And, boy, did I get an earful.

Cabina Wright was a syndicated Hollywood gossip columnist, the Luella Parsons of her time. At parties she used to corner me and ask me to dish the dirt on the stars. Like all places, Tinseltown has a little bit of everything—the good, the bad, and the ugly—but all the insider info that Cabina wanted was the bad and ugly, from diets to divorce. I guess this was how tabloids started.

I knew a great deal because people opened up to me, but I considered that a trust. I learned that from Barbara Klein who, despite her knowledge of many stars' innermost thoughts, never divulged them.

So from me Cabina heard only the good, which was certainly not grist for her mill.

You'll recall that Carol Channing and I go back to when we both attended the Elizabeth Holloway School of the Theatre in San Francisco. In 1955 I finally had the pleasure of acting with her in *Wonderful Town*, produced by Jimmy Doolittle at the Greek Theatre in Los Angeles.

That show brought me the best and worst times of my life to that point. The best were working with Carol, who was a real inspiration. The worst was the guy who played opposite me. He had an ego twice his size, believed he was irresistible to women, and couldn't keep his hands off me.

At the time I was engaged to a wonderful man, jazz guitarist Earl Colbert, and wanted no part of this egomaniac, but for the finale I was literally on his shoulders with nowhere to go.

He was ticked off at me for evading his advances and actually tried to push me off into the orchestra pit. I panicked and grabbed the first thing I could reach, his hair. Fortunately, he had his own, and lots of it, and I held on to it for dear life. After that episode, I'm sure he had a king-size headache, but that was the end of Mr. Grabby Hands.

In addition to being a talented performer, Carol was always a trouper and such a love. When I worked with her, she had very poor eyesight. To tell one actor from another, each of us in *Wonderful Town* wore a specific color on stage, so that Carol would know who we were without having to identify faces.

Opening Night — "WONDERFUL TOWN"
GREEK THEATRE — HOLLYWOOD
Produced by JAS. A. DOOLITTLE
July 6, 1955

Can you imagine what it was like for a young starlet like me to work with the great Carol Channing in this fabulous cast of "Wonderful Town"? There I am, beaming ear to ear, in the second row on the far left (just five people away from Carol).

There wasn't a selfish bone in Carol's body. She wanted us all to become stars. She even insisted on having me billed on the marquee with my name under hers. Many stars don't want other names to be displayed prominently next to theirs, especially not those of up-and-comers in the business. Carol gave her sweetness and love freely, not asking for anything in return. She was a true friend, and I have gone to see her perform every chance I get.

She never turned down an autograph-seeker, whereas I was exceptionally shy about such things. I never knew what to say to fans, but Carol said, "Don't worry." She would sign autographs on weekends when the crowds were huge, and I signed them during the week, when attendance was more sparse.

ANNIE RUDIE, THE ROCK of the DiMaggio family, flew to see me in *Wonderful Town*. It meant a lot when she told me, "Junie, you're the greatest." She actually had a beautiful contralto voice and loved to sing her favorite, "To You Sweetheart, Aloha" for everyone at the bar where she worked. They adored her, and it didn't hurt that she was also a very beautiful woman.

Since DiMaggio's opened on Fisherman's Wharf, she'd been going to work as cashier for my father, and she kept at it until she turned eighty. She was the type of woman who saw every glass as half full.

Her hobby was needlepoint. I am surrounded today by her canvasses on my walls to remind me of how encouraging and gracious she was to everyone. Marilyn once asked her if she would teach her needlepoint. Sadly, they never managed to find the time.

Annie Rudie continued to be our family's cornerstone until her passing in 1985 at the age of eighty-four. I'm grateful that she taught me so much.

IN 1956, I DID *Jeannie the WAC* and then *Ten Thousand Bedrooms* with Dean Martin, a sweet guy. I played Miss Podesta, the clerk at the jewelry store where Dino bought a ring for his girlfriend.

Although mine was a small part, Dean was very nice to me and to all of us in the cast, not treating us like underlings at all. He was always smiling and polite and tried to be helpful.

During those years, I didn't miss a beat with TV jobs, either. Work came fast and furious with series like "Lineup" and "Wyatt Earp," where I played a variety of saloon gals. The very popular Hugh O'Brien starred as the sheriff. He was lean and mean and the darling of all the young ladies.

It's well known that Hugh O'Brien had a roving eye. I was a cutie back then, and his eye roved my way more than once. On the set he

What a dame I was in saloon-girl garb, portraying a sexy siren in the TV show "Wyatt Earp." Baritone Charles Frederics joins me for a pep talk on the set.

tried to hug and kiss me. Although I knew that the script called for some action like this, he was rewriting the stage directions as we went along.

He had terrible breath, so I asked the director if he could either cut out some of our close scenes or give Hugh some breath mints. That was pretty gutsy for a youngster like me, but I wasn't afraid to say what I honestly thought, and say it out loud, too. "Tell it like it is" was the DiMaggio family motto.

Hugh O'Brien, despite getting my dressing room door slammed in his face more than once, persisted. After my scenes, he had the habit of letting himself into my room to wait for me. I was young and scared of him and his power, but I got sick and tired of the chasing game. To ward off his advances, I asked the director for a key to lock my door.

He finally got upset with my rebuffs and tried to get me fired from the series, but I got the last laugh. My cute saloon-girl character had become popular with the audience, and the powers in charge wouldn't go along with him. Role or no role, I wasn't going to be controlled by some testosterone-driven cowboy.

16

A NOT-SO-GAY DIVORCÉE

After Marilee and Uncle Joe divorced, she still met with Barbara. Since Barbara was a respected minister, Marilyn took comfort in talking with her regularly. She was interested in growing and bettering herself in all ways, from her work on the screen to her personal life, and she really took to the tenets of religious science.

In 1956 Marilyn married playwright Arthur Miller. We hadn't spoken for a while when she called me out of the blue. I could hear that she was very upset about something.

"Junie," she whispered, "I feel like the Miller family is trying to devour me."

I was totally shocked at what she confided, but listened quietly. The Miller family was pressuring her to convert to Judaism, which weighed heavily on her. She never wanted to offend anyone, but everyone seemed to either want a part of her or to change her in some way. Marilyn had always taken an interest in learning about different religions, but I sensed that she didn't want to make this major change.

One good thing Arthur Miller did for Marilyn was to encourage her to take acting lessons to better her skills. He sent her to New York to study with the famed Lee Strasberg. This, I think, was one of the most trying times of her life, yet it was also satisfying because she felt herself moving toward her dream. Unfortunately, Strasberg's daughter, Susan Strasberg, got her hands on her.

To some people, linking your name with a star's makes you feel much more important. For years Susan Strasberg went around telling everyone who would listen that she and Marilyn were the best of friends, but that's certainly not what Marilee told me confidentially. She never explained why she didn't care for Susan, but Marilyn was adamant about her dislike of her.

Marilee's longing to be a dramatic actress was never in question. After she went public about her desire to act in the screen adaptation of *The Brothers Karamazov*, she called, and we talked seriously about her attempts to get more dramatic parts, but she still didn't feel confident enough about her acting ability.

She sometimes asked me to rehearse a dramatic scene with her, knowing that I could help her achieve a deeper intensity and sensitivity—in addition to being able to serve her homemade lasagna.

Back in 1952 Marilee had starred opposite Barbara Stanwyck in *Clash by Night.* Barbara told me that Marilyn had the makings of a great actress but that she needed help with her emotional intensity, so I canceled a date, baked the lasagna, and set out to give her some one-on-one coaching on theatrical angst.

I had just finished doing a stage play, *The Rose Tattoo.* The script has some difficult emotional ups and downs in it, and I thought it was a perfect vehicle for Marilyn to practice with. In the movie version, a very young Marlon Brando costarred with Anna Magnani. There's a great dramatic scene in which Magnani runs the gamut of emotions.

I wanted Marilee to see me perform it, but I wanted her to make it her own. I worked with her to lower her voice so that she would be taken more seriously. I knew that it would have taken a giant leap for the audience if she spoke in that breathless voice she'd been using on screen. Not that she spoke that way normally, as I have said, but she just fell into it when she acted—no matter what the part.

We talked about the play. She asked me questions about motivation and how to achieve the final result. After she imitated me carefully for about an hour, we broke for dinner. When we came back to do the scene, Marilee was ready and put everything she had into it. We practiced some more. She played it over and over, trying to bring her own feelings into it.

It was getting late, but Marilee kept at it, and each time she got better. Never before had I seen her show such determination. As she was beginning the scene once more, Barbara Klein walked in and was mesmerized by Marilyn's performance. This was no longer the Marilyn Monroe the world was accustomed to on the big screen, but an accomplished dramatic actress bringing a difficult part to life.

"Bravo!" Barbara and I cried out in unison. Marilyn was thrilled to discover that she had all the talent she had dreamed of.

"Barbara talks about the soul quality in the singing voice that touches people with such emotion," Marilyn told me. "Junie, when I did that scene, I had soul quality."

That was another time I saw her cry, but with tears of happiness.

I never ceased to be amazed at the simple things Marilyn didn't know or never got to learn. Barbara and I even had to teach her how to set a table properly. I suspect that because she was a star, chores like that were done for her. You'd think that she would have learned some of that during her childhood in foster homes, but Marilee was serious about learning the correct way. Her drive for perfection carried through into everything she did.

I drove her back to her apartment that night. Whenever Marilyn needed a ride home, either I drove her or a limousine picked her up. I'm sure she could have had all the cars she wanted, but I never saw her drive.

I was happy for her and thought she must be exhausted from all her work that night, but her adrenaline was flowing. She went on and on about how she felt about what she'd accomplished that night. I wanted her to go back to her own coach at 20th Century Fox to show what progress she'd made. I hoped that the woman would let those in charge know how Marilyn had grown and perhaps convince them it was time to take her seriously. I doubt that Marilee slept much that night.

She later told me what happened the next day. Awakening with the assurance that she could be the dramatic actress she had always dreamed of being, she dressed quickly to get an early start. She walked into 20th Century with all her dreams before her. Now that she could accomplish more roles on the screen than ever before, how could they turn her down?

Sadly, Marilyn soon realized that the movie moguls didn't want her to blossom into the best actress that she could be. The profits that they were making from her work were too huge. They told her in no uncertain terms that she was a sex symbol, and a sex symbol she would remain on their screens. It reminded me of Ann Sothern's earlier fight to be taken seriously.

That executive brush-off left Marilyn shaken, questioning who she really was and crushing what belief in herself that she had.

I feel even today that Marilyn had the same ability as Meryl Streep. She could be funny one minute, deep and poignant the next. To me it seemed absurd that anyone could doubt her ability as a credible actress. All that they needed to do would have been to check out her performance in *Don't Bother Knocking*, a low-budget movie released in 1952. In it she played Nell Forbes, the niece of a New York hotel elevator man who lands her the job of babysitting the daughter of a married couple staying at the hotel. Marilyn is convincing and frightening in the role as she comes apart before your very eyes—almost too convincing. She told me that she had used memories of her mother's instability to help her make the role real.

She longed to do drama, and she could do it well, but typecast as the sexy blonde, Marilyn's true acting brilliance remained hidden to most moviegoers.

At Christmas Barbara and I used to go all out with decorations and parties and presents galore. In southern California, people joke that the only way you know it's winter is when you change the plastic flowers. To display the cards we got from family and friends, I strung a clothesline across our dining room, attaching the cards to it with old-fashioned wooden clothespins. In this age of fiber optics and computer-generated images, it might sound silly, but back then it seemed special and distinctive. I still do it to this day.

As the 25th of December approached, that clothesline grew more crowded. It was never fancy, but all who visited could see how much we cherished their greetings.

Just a few days before Christmas, Marilyn made one of her impromptu late-afternoon visits, and we invited her to stay for dinner. She bounded into our living room and stopped in her tracks like a little kid seeing the lights on the Christmas tree for a first time.

"Oh," she said, staring at the dining room clothesline hung with all our cards. "I wish I would get cards like that so I could put up a clothesline like yours."

"Don't you get any cards?" I asked.

I couldn't imagine Marilyn Monroe not getting Christmas cards! She looked at me and said that she didn't. "Oh, I guess I get them at the studio, but I never see them," she said. "They're from people I don't know."

She stood there for a long time, oohing and aahing over each card. I'm sure the studio's publicity department received cards for her from thousands of fans, but even if they took the trouble to acknowledge them, they never passed them along, and Marilyn never got to see them personally.

Marilyn was so mesmerized by the clothesline that our food was getting cold and I had to almost drag her away. We had a wonderful dinner, laughing and talking about work. Marilyn made me laugh when she described some of the escapades she had with her costars.

When she was making the Otto Preminger movie *River of No Return* with Robert Mitchum, they were on a rough river on a homemade barge.

Marilyn told us how deathly afraid she was since she was not a strong swimmer. She told us that Robert Mitchum had assured her that he'd take care of her, including if she fell into the river—which she didn't.

The next day I couldn't get Marilyn's enjoyment of my card clothesline off my mind. Then I had an idea. I went into a drawer and pulled out about a dozen different unused cards from Christmases past and wrote a different message, some serious, others silly, on each one. Using my left hand to write, so she wouldn't recognize my penmanship, I signed them with all the phony names I could think of. I slid them into a large manila envelope and addressed it *To Marilyn*. I didn't add a personal note because I wanted her to be surprised.

I dropped the envelope off at her back door. If getting Christmas cards would help her feel just like everyone else, I was glad to deliver some.

I had a date later that evening, so what I'd done slipped my mind until the next morning when the phone rang. It was Marilyn, so excited she almost couldn't speak.

"Junie, Junie!" she said. "I got cards! Please come over and see my cards."

I went, and she met me at the door with not a dab of makeup on; she was beautiful still, but it was not the gorgeously groomed face of her publicity shots. I barely had time to say hello before she grabbed my arm and dragged me inside. Stretched across her living room was a clothesline with my dozen cards hanging from it—each one secured with her silver and gold hair clips.

She couldn't stop talking proudly about the wonderful spectacle and how she put up the clothesline all by herself, how thrilled she was. She went on and on, filled with joy over just a few cards.

I still hang my Christmas clothesline every year and think about how we never know what kind of impact we can have on people with a simple action. It's the simple things we do that often matter most.

17

PAINFUL PREMONITIONS

I'VE EXPERIENCED EPISODES of ESP throughout my life, but I never had and still have absolutely no control over them. Extrasensory perception picks you; not the other way around.

Reva Frederick, the brain behind actor Robert Mitchum, lived next door to us in Hollywood. One day I felt the need to go to her office on Sunset Boulevard. I had come to do what I felt compelled to do when I felt this way and no longer questioned that feeling.

Stepping into her office, I had a vision of Reva lying on the floor and knew immediately that she would suffer a diabetic coma. When the vision passed, there was Reva talking with her friend Gloria. Both of them seemed fine, but all of a sudden, Reva staggered just a bit.

I ordered her to call the doctor. She laughed at me, but seeing how distressed I was, she finally relented and made an appointment. The doctor took one look at her and off to the hospital she went. I was right; she had diabetes.

After that incident, Reva and I became close friends. Later she married a producer. When she became pregnant, the doctors warned her that because of her diabetes the baby might be born deformed and she might die.

She desperately wanted a baby, and she came to me in tears. Remember, this was before sonograms, but when I turned and looked at her, I could actually see inside her body, baby and all.

161

I told her, "You're going to have a beautiful little baby girl who's going to be happy and healthy. And you're going to give her a funny name, too. It'll start with an *M* and end in *kah*, or something like that." As it turned out, she named her Malka, in honor of her husband's mother.

After that near tragedy, Reva heeded my every warning. When she was supposed to fly to New York to sign a contract for a picture with Robert Mitchum, I told her to wait for the next flight out of Los Angeles.

"The one you're scheduled to take is going down in the water in New York," I said. "There will be no deaths, but it's going down."

Reva didn't question my advice this time. She canceled her flight. Later she called to tell me that the plane she would have been on had, indeed, crashed as it was landing in New York. As I'd predicted, there were no deaths, but there were many injuries.

Still, not everyone listened to me. Even my own father was a skeptic at first. I described to him a condition I saw that he had, but didn't know what to call it.

"It's like you can see only what's in front of you," I told him. "You need to get glasses."

He didn't believe me, but after my prodding, he went to the eye doctor. Sure enough, he was diagnosed with a condition that could be helped with glasses. To let me know I'd been right on target, he mailed me a snapshot of himself wearing his new glasses. Father never doubted me again.

❧

NOT ALL MY ESP EXPERIENCES were well received. One of Barbara Klein's students was Mary Anderson, one of the actresses afloat with Tallulah Bankhead in Alfred Hitchcock's *Lifeboat.* Mary's husband, Leon Shamroy, was an ace photographer for 20th Century Fox who was shooting

My father, Tom DiMaggio, proudly shows off his eyeglasses after I used my ESP to diagnose him with an eye problem.

a film on Harold Sherman, the world-renowned authority on ESP and author of the definitive bestseller *TNT: The Power Within You.*

At the height of his popularity, Sherman was as popular as rock stars are today. In 1958 Mary introduced me to him at the Wilshire Ebell Theatre in Hollywood. He did his full stage presentation as I sat mesmerized. After the show, a huge line gathered to get his autograph. I don't know what came over me, but I walked past all those standing in line and right up to Sherman and said, "I'm June DiMaggio, and you're going to call me." I gave him my phone number and slipped away.

Perhaps it was the shock of my being so bold, or maybe he was a little curious about that last name of DiMaggio, but he did call, and it changed my life.

*It was on the stage of the Wilshire Ebell in
Los Angeles that I learned that Harold
Sherman wanted to be the ESP star, and I
was stealing his thunder.*

I was totally open and honest with him.

"I don't know anything about this parapsychology thing," I said,
"but we are going to see a spaceship together on a rooftop."

He startled me by replying that he, too, thought he would see a
spaceship on a rooftop, but that he would be alone at the time.

Then I sort of forgot about it.

A few days later we both happened to be on the roof of the
Chateau Marmont, a popular Hollywood hotel, where Harold Sherman

and his wife Martha were staying. The apartment I shared with Barbara was just across the street. We talked about ESP and our experiences. After an hour, it was time for me to go. I had an early stage call at the studio the next morning. I also had a date that evening that I was looking forward to.

When I got home, it was nearing midnight. Just as I was about to enter my apartment, I was drawn to look up into the dark sky. I couldn't believe my eyes and quickly ran back across the street to the Marmont. I just knew Harold would be on the roof as he had predicted, and I wasn't mistaken.

He was as stunned as I was. There in the sky was a tubular spaceship belching out lavender smoke, like something in a scene from *Star Trek*. Harold and I stood transfixed, gazing in awe and experiencing it together, just as I had predicted. After a few minutes, the ship zipped away into the dark night. Neither he nor I spoke; we didn't need to. Then we went our separate ways in silence.

Somehow the word got around, and eventually the Air Force from the local base invited us to share what we had seen. It was all hush-hush, but they showed us films they had taken of the event. The military planes tracking this huge spaceship looked like little ants. Sherman and I were both written up in a significant ESP journal reporting this experience, but not much came of it. In those days so much was kept quiet, and the Air Force kept it so.

That was the start of my brief professional relationship with Harold Sherman. I became involved with him and Thelma Moss at UCLA, where Thelma held classes about parapsychology and performed experiments in mental telepathy. I appeared on stage with Sherman several times, but our collaboration was short lived.

ONCE WHEN SHERMAN AND I were both on stage, I couldn't stop myself from shouting into the audience, "Evelyn, please call your home because your house is on fire." A woman, evidently by that name, went rushing out of the theatre.

I took a deep breath and hoped for the best. A short time later, the woman returned and thanked me profusely. A fire had indeed started in her house, and had she not telephoned, she would have lost everything.

But Harold Sherman was the star of that show. He felt I was showing him up, that I'd made a bigger impact than he did, so my stage career with this egotistical man came to an end soon afterward.

As it happened, that very night Gloria Swanson was in the audience. She was interested in metaphysics as well as in Barbara Klein's vocal coaching. Duly impressed, she invited Barbara, Harold, and me to her Bel Air estate.

Harold was supposed to be the guest of honor, but as we sat on the gorgeous patio of her exclusive home, Gloria asked me about my ESP powers. I explained that it was just a part of me, like breathing. I had no power over it; either it came to me or it didn't. She seemed more interested in my telling her things than she was in asking Harold. When she said she wanted to see me again, I was flattered, but didn't know what I could do for her.

Even though Gloria was older—she had just portrayed Desdemona, the over-the-hill star in *Sunset Boulevard*—I still thought of her as sexy.

In my outspoken way, I asked her, "Why do you have so many obviously gay boys running around the house?" I didn't mind either way, but I was curious.

Her explanation surprised me.

"They run errands and do anything I ask them, just to be around me," she said.

She probably found it comfortable to have them around, not having to worry about their having any sexual interest in her. At her home that first time, I didn't ask any more questions, but through ESP I perceived that she had a lover, and told her so.

"You are involved with a very young man," I said. "You could be his mother."

Gloria's eyes opened wide.

Evidently she knew exactly who I meant. I was afraid she was getting into a situation she wouldn't be able to handle. I knew that this young man wasn't going to stay very long. It was her notoriety that drew him to her, certainly not real love. After all, he was much, much younger.

"It's not right," I went on. "Send him on his way."

I told her it would end unhappily for her, and it wasn't worth it, and Gloria followed my instructions and gave him his walking papers.

I knew Gloria for about a year and a half. I shared with her what impressions I could, but never again got the strong feelings I did about that one young love in her life.

What tangled lives these stars led! Their search for answers and true love was ongoing, but in Hollywood it was so difficult to decipher what was real and what was simply Hollywood.

MARY ANDERSON HAD definitely started the ball rolling for my association with Harold Sherman, but unfortunately she figured in one of the more tragic experiences I had with ESP.

I returned home after a singing engagement, and I knew one of my episodes was coming on because I broke into a sweat. I both saw and felt an extremely painful scenario that seemed to be my responsibility to tell Mary, regardless of the consequences.

I had met her father briefly, but now I told her that I saw him turning on a car ignition.

"He has diabetes. His doctor told him he has to quit drinking, and no more sweets, either," I told her, sensing drinking and sweets were two things that he was fond of. "He doesn't want to live that way, and in ten days he's going to commit suicide. You have to stop him."

Mary laughed at me, but I begged her to take me seriously. Then she grew angry and screamed, "Are you trying to tell me you know this from a perception?"

I insisted that she call her father and ask him straight out if he had been diagnosed with diabetes. She did, but he lied and told her, "No way."

In a less-than-pleasant tone of voice, she told me to drop the subject, but I couldn't, because I had more to tell her.

"You are going to sign a contract to be in a movie with George Raft. But please," I pleaded, "don't sign it, because you're not going to finish the movie and your father will die while you're away."

Mary was startled, but told me the picture was a done deal and that she was leaving in one week to start the film. I begged her not to go and to stay with her father.

"He needs you now," I said. "Besides, the movie isn't going to be successful."

She wouldn't listen and, as planned, she left to begin shooting on location.

I hoped I would be wrong, but I was devastated when ten days later she got the fateful call and had to rush back home. Her father had gone into the garage, turned on the car's ignition, and died from carbon monoxide poisoning.

He left a note telling his family that after learning that he had diabetes and would have to live such a restricted life, he just couldn't go on.

I tried to tell Mary I'd only wanted to spare her pain, not cause her any more, but I could see the loathing in her eyes. She called me a witch and said she never wanted to see me again. Our friendship ended then and there.

The movie she had begun shooting folded before it was ever in the can, so all that I'd predicted for her came true. From then on, I promised Barbara that I would never tell anyone what I perceived unless it was good. My predictions of bad news lost me good friends and brought me great pain.

But sometimes the ending was happy.

Barbara's friends, the Kirkpatrick family, called me because their young son was setting fires and killing animals and they were at their wit's end. Since they were Barbara's friends, I couldn't refuse them.

I met with their son Robert and played some mental telepathy games, asking him to identify objects I had in mind, and he was right on. As our conversation continued, Robert began to trust me and opened up about "the thing" he had inside him. I was shocked, but didn't let on and pushed him to explain.

He said it was the devil.

"But he looks like a man," Robert said. "He comes in me and pushes me to do terrible things."

I was flabbergasted, but, not about to give up, I asked Robert to send me telepathic messages when we were apart, especially when that devil man came calling. I also instructed him to write down the messages he got every Wednesday, precisely at 10 A.M. I told him that I would, too, and we would then mail the messages to each other.

I felt wary. Would he be able to read too many of my inner thoughts? I couldn't block them, but I was determined to help this beautiful little boy.

Our exercises continued for the better part of a year. Slowly but surely, he stopped doing those terrible things. Working with him left me exhausted, but really pleased. Robert grew up to be a fine young man who served in Vietnam and came home a hero.

Word got out about what I had done. Hearing of the success I had with Robert, other friends of his family called on me, desperate because their son had been kidnapped. He needed asthma medication and time was running out. Police had no clue, and they hoped that I could find him.

They sent me one of the dirty, sand-covered tee-shirts he had worn just before his disappearance. As I touched the shirt, I went into a semi-drowsy state and suddenly blurted out, "I know where he is!"

Everyone was startled, but to me it seemed clear as crystal.

"He's in Connecticut on a farm," I said. "He is with an old man with a beard. There's a big dog with him, a Saint Bernard. There is a huge barn with the words 'My Red Barn' written on it."

I learned that the police had searched on the East Coast, but not in Connecticut.

I confidently told his family, "You'll have your son back in three days."

As they waited anxiously, they stayed with me in Los Angeles.

In three days, sure enough, the police located him and immediately rushed him to the hospital. It seems the old man I'd seen had no grandson and had kidnapped the little boy—just nine years old—to fill that need. He told the child, "Your parents want you to vacation on my farm." He didn't harm the boy, but he also didn't know about the child's asthma.

His parents were overjoyed, but the police suspected I might be in on the kidnapping. When they came to ask how I could possibly know all this, I honestly told them. "I used my God-given ability with ESP."

They remained suspicious, but fortunately Reva Frederick came to my rescue. She explained that my ability was legitimate and that she had experienced wonderful results. Besides, I had never accepted money for my predictions.

Still, this case took its toll on me. During that time, I was still doing TV shows like "Lineup" and "Wyatt Earp," which alone were tiring. I telephoned Barbara from the set, telling her how happy I was that the boy was found but that I never wanted to do this again. I just couldn't handle my own life along with the hell of other peoples' traumas. I vowed this would be the last time I got so involved.

I never went public again, but the ability never really went away. Even today I deal with this gift and curse from time to time and I still keep that sandy, dirty little tee-shirt as a remembrance.

18

one troublesome young man, one troubled actress

ONE DAY IN 1960 Joe DiMaggio Junior came to Barbara's and my Hollywood apartment with a girl in tow to tell us they had gotten married. He and his new bride, a model, were both just eighteen.

As became a theme throughout his sad life, Joe actually wanted something more than just to tell us the good news. This time he wanted me to give him money and to tell his mother about his marriage.

When I called Dorothy, she came to the apartment and told her son and his bride bluntly that they were on their own. She really seemed at the end of her rope with her son and didn't know what else to do but to try tough love.

Even being cut off, Joe Junior wouldn't get a job, and his new wife wasn't about to support them. After a month the marriage was annulled.

Joe Junior never seemed to get his act together and wandered aimlessly through life. He never felt that his father was there for him; Uncle Joe was always on the road. He sent wonderful and expensive gifts for every occasion, but they didn't make up for his not being present for his little boy.

As a result, Joe Junior was always angry and at odds with his father. I was there for many of his birthdays. He actually refused to open his father's presents until his mother forced him to.

You would think Joe Junior would have inherited some of his father's sports ability, but all that he seemed to share with his famous dad was his temper. I remember him losing it with me on the tennis court once. I was a pretty good player and beat the tennis shorts off of him when he was about twelve. He threw a tantrum and flung his racket toward me with real venom.

Being a poor sport was the tip of the iceberg. He had problems. Even though he never wanted for anything, nothing ever seemed right to him. Dorothy, realizing that he needed more discipline, enrolled Joe Junior in military school, hoping it would straighten him out, but eventually he was expelled.

The family really tried hard to look after Joe Junior. Joe's brother Dominic gave him a job in his fiberglass company, but ultimately had to fire him.

Once when Joe was visiting my parents, Joe Junior called and wanted to meet with his father. He told me he wanted his father to buy him a truck for work. I urged Uncle Joe to buy it for him. "Give him a chance, Joe," I told him. Both of us assumed it was to be a pickup truck, so Uncle Joe agreed. A few months later Joe got the bill for a refrigerated tractor-trailer truck costing huge bucks even for the well-off Joe DiMaggio. His son wanted it, he said, to transport frozen food to the U.S. from Mexico. In the end, Joe Junior totaled the new truck, knocking out his front teeth in the process and costing his father another $10,000 to cover the damage. Suffice it to say that I told Uncle Joe I'd never try to interfere again.

No real father-son relationship ever grew between the two men, but Joe Senior always had a soft spot for children. He established the Joe DiMaggio Children's Hospital at Memorial Regional Hospital in Hollywood, Florida, in 1992.

Joe Junior married again, to a woman with two little girls from a previous marriage. To no one's surprise, this match didn't work out either, but Uncle Joe adopted his son's two stepdaughters after his son walked out on that family, and he left his estate to the girls when he died.

As for Joe Junior, he remained a troubled and not very nice man. His mother adored him and showered him with love and attention all his life, yet he didn't even attend her funeral. He did attend Marilyn's service, walking in full-dress Marine uniform next to his father, but that was all for show. His estrangement from his father continued, and he spent much of his life living on the streets. He ultimately ended up in a broken-down trailer when alcohol and unchecked asthma took their toll and he died in 1999 at age fifty-seven, just a few months after his father died.

After her divorce from Joe, Dorothy married a stockbroker in New York, but that marriage lasted just a few months. She finally found happiness in her third marriage to a really great guy. They married in Palm Springs, where he operated a gay bar. Dorothy sang there for many years and loved her work. She remained beautiful and sexy until she died of cancer at age sixty-six.

MARILEE WAS SO DIFFERENT from the DiMaggio family, especially when her sensitive side surfaced. She often came to our apartment when she was feeling vulnerable or blue. Barbara and I had all sorts of knick-knacks—souvenirs of places we had visited and gifts from family and friends—like my beer steins from Jeanette MacDonald and trinkets from Hoagy Carmichael.

One of Barbara's keepsakes was a cute little teddy bear that enjoyed a prominent place in our living room. On this particular day, Barbara caught Marilyn looking longingly at the stuffed animal. It seemed odd for a little teddy bear to capture Marilyn's attention, but she confided to Barbara that she (who ironically could now buy herself anything in the world) had never had a teddy bear in her whole life. I found that incredible and thought she must be kidding. Doesn't every child have a teddy bear or stuffed critter at sometime or other? But Marilyn was telling the truth.

The next day, I got off work from a TV program and met Marilyn coming up the walkway of our apartment. She told me that Barbara had left word for her to drop by after she left the studio. Her message read, "Your child is waiting for you."

We went in and found a grinning Barbara, who had been plotting the surprise all day. She'd persuaded Georgia Maxwell, Hoagy Carmichael's sister, to go to Robinson's, the department store on Wilshire Boulevard, and buy two teddy bears because she didn't have time. Then Barbara dressed them with five-and-dime pearl necklaces.

I still hug this wonderful teddy bear (Marilyn called her Barbie Bear), knowing how much it meant to Marilyn. It makes me feel closer to her once again.

One bear was white, which Barbara gave to me. The other, with golden-brown fur, went to Marilyn. Marilyn clutched that bear to her, saying that she loved it and was going to call her "Barbie Bear."

Marilyn sang that diamonds are a girl's best friend, but that stuffed bear meant more to her than all the diamonds in the world. It remained in her bedroom until the end.

I remember Marilyn's bedroom after she died as if it were a photograph in my mind. I just knew Barbie Bear was there as a sad reminder of this woman-child who had suffered so much and asked for so little.

In the early hours of the morning after her death, I went back to Marilyn's house and used the key to the back door that she had given me to let myself in. I took back the teddy bear and the pizza pan that I'd brought the day of her death, and left.

Whenever I look at that teddy bear, wearing the same dime-store pearls, I remember the gentle woman who loved life so much and was so misunderstood.

19

sweet mystery no more

SHOW PEOPLE ARE superstitious and often look for explanations for their complicated lives. That's why so many of my friends came to me for my ESP abilities. Jeanette MacDonald was also very much interested in ESP, and so she held a dinner party inviting all her friends who wanted to know more about the subject. Her stunning, high-ceilinged house was done all in pink with exquisite furniture—just the tasteful décor that you'd expect from this beautiful person.

This night, after her husband Gene opened the doors to the party room, down the spiral staircase glided Jeanette in a pink satin gown, color-coordinated with her hair. Glamour personified, she was around sixty by this time, but could have passed for thirty. An aura shimmered around her, as if light emanated from her being.

With all eyes on her, she came directly to me. "Ladies and gentlemen," she announced, "I want you all to meet my friend, June Bug."

Of course, I loved that she called me by my nickname.

Jeanette's sister, Blossom Seely, was there, too, as were architect Frank Lloyd Wright, actor Lloyd Nolan, and MGM producer Joe Pasternak. But where was Nelson Eddy? He and Jeanette had acted in so many movies together, and I was curious why he wasn't at her party. Jeanette politely explained to me that he was a screen hog. He never shot a scene where he wasn't the focal point, she said, and she was none too fond of him.

There was, however, one actor she absolutely adored working with—Maurice Chevalier. She added quickly that she had performed with him before her marriage to Gene, which led me to wonder if theirs had been more than just a working relationship.

The party was a joy. I went on about Harold Sherman and how we met, and I shared all I could about ESP. Suddenly, I had to stop. I knew what was coming over me. It had happened to me this way ever since childhood. I got feelings about where a missing child could be found, or I saw what was going to happen to someone, but never knew when or where it was going to happen.

I became very quiet, my heart raced, and I broke into a cold sweat. I had a premonition, but one I didn't want to believe.

"I don't want to tell Jeanette what I am feeling," I whispered to Barbara Klein, there with me.

"It's your obligation to give her the information," Barbara said.

When I asked to speak with Jeanette alone, she could see how upset I was. She brought me into the bathroom. I was shaking like a leaf.

"Please, Jeanette," I pleaded, "don't go to Texas for that operation."

"How could you know?" she asked, astonished. "Only Gene knows about my heart surgery. I have to go."

I started to cry. "Please don't go," I repeated.

Jeanette tried to comfort me to no avail.

"Fix your face and we will talk later," she told me.

What she didn't know was that I realized she would not make it through the operation. My idol was going to die, and I was hysterical.

As she asked me to, I returned to the party, where I told Barbara that I couldn't tell Jeanette everything; it was too painful. Barbara told me to start by giving Gene the information.

The dinner we had was beautiful, but I was still haunted, because this evening premonitions were coming fast and just wouldn't let me go. I turned to Jeanette's sister Blossom.

"You're going to New York," I said, "to be in a play called *Blossom Time*."

Surprised, she said, "Yes." Apparently no one had yet heard the news.

"Don't go," I continued. "You won't do the play and you'll just waste your time and money." I knew the show would fold before it ever opened.

Even her husband said, "I told you so, Blossom."

Then I turned to Frank Lloyd Wright's wife.

"You're going to a wedding," I said, knowing it was her cousin's wedding. "And you're having difficulty finding a gown. Don't worry; the bride has chosen gowns for her bridesmaids. You must wear what she wants you to. Just take back whatever you got."

You can imagine the looks I got from both of these ladies as I spoke. As it turned out, I was right on all counts. *Blossom Time* never opened, and the wedding of Frank Lloyd Wright's cousin-in-law turned out just fine.

I was extremely upset that night when we went home. I told Barbara that I hated picking up bad premonitions, especially for people that I loved and admired so much.

Barbara, ever practical, called Gene and explained to him how distraught I was and how I had perceived that Jeanette would die in Texas on the operating table.

Gene explained that Jeanette had some sort of artery problem in her neck and needed the procedure. Before the fateful surgery, she called me one more time and said, "June Bug, you've been such a joy."

I burst into tears, telling her how it had been the greatest thrill just to know her.

"I would give anything if you wouldn't go for the operation," I begged.

She asked me not to cry and to please say a prayer for her.

Just before her operation, I got to see Jeanette one final time.

She wanted to shoot one more movie before the surgery and came to see Barbara to prepare for the role. They were in another room. I sat at the piano thinking that I wanted to do something for Jeanette. I called out to Barbara and said that I wanted to sing "Ah, Sweet Mystery of Life." I knew that this would be the last time I saw Jeanette, and I wanted her to hear me do the same song she'd sung for me the first time we met.

Barbara reminded me that I had never sung that song by myself or ever worked on it with her, but I knew it thoroughly because I associated it with Jeanette, and I couldn't let this last chance go by.

Barbara called Jeanette to the piano and told her, "I have a special performance for you."

I wanted to sing like an angel for this angel of a lady. My heart raced as Barbara began playing the introduction.

I sang for all I was worth.

Jeanette had tears in her eyes. When I finished the song, she rose from the chair, took my hand, and began to sing with me.

When we finished, I just stood there not knowing what else to say. Gently she put her arms around me and kissed me.

"That was beautiful," she said softly.

It was a moment that I have cherished and remembered all my life.

As to my premonition, all my warnings and laments were to no avail. Jeanette had made up her mind. She went to Texas for surgery. I knew she wouldn't make it. My idol, my friend, the woman who inspired me to my life's work, died as I had perceived. She was just sixty-one years old.

I vowed never to perceive again; precognition brought me only pain and anguish, especially since I couldn't change the outcome, but I have treasured the times I had with this extraordinary, spiritual lady.

AFTER MARILYN DIVORCED Arthur Miller, she fell into a deep depression. It appeared that her life and career were finally taking their toll. Her psychiatrist wanted to admit her to a facility where she could work out her problems, but Marilee was too afraid. Several times she'd told me that she was terrified at the thought of the "booby hatch," as she called it.

Not long after she was born, her mother had a nervous breakdown and was institutionalized for the rest of her days. Marilyn realized it wasn't her mother's fault that she was mentally ill, but she was clearly frightened that her mother's fate might be her inherited destiny as well.

Marilyn had good reason to be afraid of what might happen to her.

I never got all the details, but before she realized it, Marilyn was in a padded cell at New York's Payne-Whitney Psychiatric Clinic with no way out.

After being admitted, Marilyn called the one person she trusted. Although it had been several years since their divorce, it was Uncle Joe she looked to for help. Joe still loved and adored Marilyn. His feelings never changed even after their divorce. That's why he never married again.

Receiving her call, Joe went to get her. It didn't hurt that *the* Joe DiMaggio was making the demand. He threatened those who had committed her with lawsuits or worse and told them that he would take down the building brick by brick if she weren't released immediately. With Joe's clout, Marilyn was out in no time. Joe took her to a regular hospital, where she swiftly recovered from exhaustion.

FOR THE LAST TWO YEARS of her life, in particular, Marilyn and I were once again close.

On one of her visits to us in Beverly Hills, she was very upset with her voice coach at 20th Century Fox because her training wasn't progressing under this teacher's tutelage. She wanted to become better in all aspects of her work, but she didn't seem to be improving at all.

Always glad to help, Barbara discovered that Marilyn had a tiny voice with a small range, but Barbara said that didn't matter. She advised Marilyn to keep her songs in the middle range, and showed her how to work with what she had to sound great. She always taught her pupils that using what they had to the fullest, with the strength that comes from deep inside, is more important than the notes that come out of the voice box.

Marilyn worked hard to be the best she could, listened to every word Barbara said, and took it all to heart. Armed with Barbara's good advice, she returned to her coach, and from then on, made major strides with her vocals.

Do you remember Marilyn singing "Happy Birthday" to President John Kennedy at his forty-fifth birthday party in Washington on May 29, 1962? That special performance almost didn't take place.

She had been terribly ill for several days with a sore throat, laryngitis, and a fever over 100 degrees. Marilyn didn't have the energy or the voice for singing and begged to stay home. Her singing voice was not the best, and feeling ill, she knew that it was next to impossible to pull off this performance. But 20th Century Fox officials ordered her to perform that night.

Marilyn called Barbara for help, and Barbara telephoned Marilyn's voice coach at Fox. The coach came to our apartment and disagreed with Barbara. She wanted Marilyn to sing the song in a high key. Barbara prevailed and lowered the song two full keys and insisted that Marilyn "talk" the song.

Marilyn gave Barbara Klein this autographed pin-up poster. She loved Barbara for the friendship they shared and Barbara's spiritual counseling and vocal coaching.

I took a different tack to help. I had Marilyn gargle with red wine vinegar, salt, and water, using an old Italian sore throat remedy. She could hardly stand it—and it sounds terrible—but I use that gargle even today, and I've never missed a performance.

Since Marilee had no choice but to do what the studio said, she stayed at our apartment overnight, working to achieve a vocal style that would get her through the performance. Barbara told her she was going to do the song like a sexy chanteuse—more spoken, breathy, and whispery than outright singing.

By the time she had to leave, I could see the worry on her face, but I knew that Marilyn would pull it off.

I watched the television anxiously to see how things turned out. When she got up to the podium, she did exactly what Barbara had told her to do—she sang "Happy Birthday" in her breathiest, sexiest voice.

And the audience loved it.

How many thousands of times have we heard the song that almost never was? Barbara Klein made magic for Marilyn—and the world—that night, transforming what could have been a major disappointment into a historical success.

All the press talked about or cared about was how Marilyn had been "poured into" or sewn into the glitter gown she wore that evening. I can tell you, the dress had a zipper. Yes, it was formfitting, but so what? That was part of her image. Still, Marilyn never protested the reports.

AT A PARTY ONE NIGHT a few years later, I ran into Barbara Stanwyck, who acted with Marilyn in *Clash by Night*.

I just walked up to her and said, "Hi, Bo" and asked if she believed in ESP. Barbara sort of shrugged her shoulders, but she listened. I went on about a television series that I felt was coming into her future, something with the word *valley* in it.

"Yes!" she exclaimed. "It's called 'The Big Valley.'" After she collected herself and we chatted more, she asked if I'd be interested in playing the part of her daughter on the series.

I thanked her very much, but said no. I was a singer at heart, and I knew I had to follow my own dream. As you know, Linda Evans eventually got the role.

As the evening progressed, she and I kept up an on-again, off-again conversation. Finally she asked, "Are you going to sing this evening?"

I was flattered. "What's your favorite musical?" I asked. It was *Finian's Rainbow,* and she particularly loved the song "How Are Things in Gloccamorra?" Hoagy played for me, and I sang.

Afterward Barbara Stanwyck hugged me and turned to walk away.

"Don't ride any horses," I blurted out, unable to stop myself. "You're going to fall off and get a permanent injury that will plague you all your life."

Barbara stopped in her tracks to face me. She laughed softly and started to leave.

"Please don't laugh, because I won't see you again for a long time," I said. "I'm telling you the truth."

I went on to tell her that I also saw the number ten. "Please be careful," I begged.

She apologized for not paying attention and put her arms around me to comfort me.

I couldn't understand why people wouldn't heed my warnings. I hadn't asked for this gift—or curse—of ESP, and I offered the information that came to me freely and with an open heart.

On the set of "The Big Valley" just ten months later, Barbara Stanwyck did indeed fall off a horse and was permanently injured.

Barbara Stanwyck always sent thank-you notes to Barbara Klein and me, even for the littlest things. Here's one that I treasure.

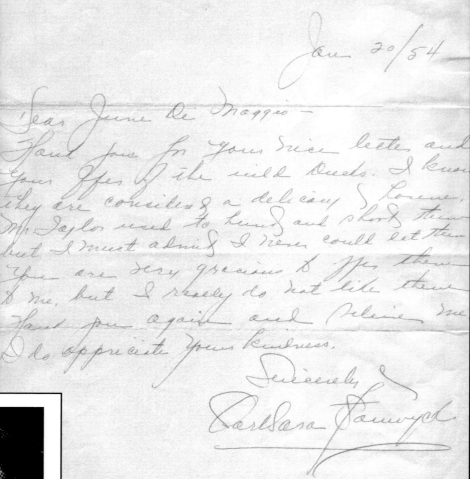

My "Bo." Barbara Stanwyck remained my friend until her death. I always loved it when she called me "June Bug."

June 20/54

Dear June DiMaggio—
Thank you for your nice letter and your offer of the wild ducks. I know they are considered a delicacy. However, Mr. Taylor used to hunt and shoot terns, but I must admit I never could eat them. You are very gracious to offer them to me, but I really do not like them. Thank you again and believe me, I do appreciate your kindness.

Sincerely,
Barbara Stanwyck

Bo, who had begun her career as a chorus girl at age seventeen, completed ninety-three movies in her career. She and I kept in touch over the years, until just a few days before her passing, when I got a call that she wanted to see me.

She was on kidney dialysis. I could see that these were her final days.

She told me how difficult it had been to be a star and how one could feel so used. She wanted me to know that the life of a celebrity can be very lonely. She told me of awful instances how, throughout her career, directors and producers pursued her, and that even in her later years younger types thought they could make a conquest of her and take some of her celebrity.

"When you come to the twilight of your life, June Bug, you are fortunate if you can count five friends," she said. "I can count four. You are one."

Those were her last words to me.

20

A Crime That's Still Unsolved

On August 4, 1962, Marilyn died.

I'm asked over and over, did she really commit suicide? I know for a fact that *Marilyn was murdered.* There is no doubt in my mind.

On the very day of her death, Marilyn phoned me mid-morning and asked if I could bring her one of my homemade pizzas. I had a tennis date planned, but I never refused Marilyn if I thought she needed me, even if it was just for some girl talk and pizza. When I arrived with the pizza around noon, she was in high spirits, chatting about how she and my mother were going to Mexico to shop for wrought-iron patio furniture for the new home where she and Joe would live after they remarried.

Yes, remarried. They were planning to retie the knot on August 8, the day that would instead be her funeral.

Marilyn was very happy and excited to be marrying Joe again. She was even thinking of domestic comforts and bought a set of dishes for their new love nest. I know, because they were left to me, and I kept those dishes for many years after she died.

When I saw her that fateful day, she went on and on about her new life and her plans for the future. She also intimated that she wanted to slow down a bit in the business. She had a contract to fulfill, but she was hoping to cut back to perhaps a movie a year so that she could finally begin to enjoy life with her own family, in her own cozy home.

Marilyn loved her work and she loved challenges, but she was contemplating some big changes with a happy heart. I cannot believe that she would commit suicide when she was looking ahead with such anticipation.

Joe had made it clear that he had learned his lesson. There would be no more silent treatment. I believe that he'd come to realize that Marilyn couldn't become the matronly Italian housewife he thought he wanted the first time around, and that he was okay with that because he loved her so deeply. I knew that Marilyn was Joe's real love. From the way she was beaming that day, I saw firsthand that Marilyn, too, was thrilled to be starting over with Joe.

On the night that she was murdered, the police were trying to locate Joe to tell him that she'd been found dead. Unable to find him right away, they knocked at my door between 11 P.M. and midnight and told me what had happened. I had returned after my date sometime between 10 and 11 P.M. When I heard the news, I went into shock. I couldn't believe what they were telling me, and I didn't know where Joe was for sure, so I called to ask Mother. I remember thinking that he might be in San Francisco. When she picked up the phone, Mother was sobbing uncontrollably.

She already knew.

Marilyn had been talking with her on the phone, Mother told me, when intruders entered Marilyn's house. In her terror, Marilyn dropped the phone, but the killers never hung it up. Mother told me that she had heard it all—the voices in the room, the struggle, the silence. All accounts that I know of state that when Marilyn was found, her phone was still off the hook.

How did the police know to come to me? I can only guess that Mother dialed 0 for the operator, got connected to the San Francisco police, who immediately called the Los Angeles authorities. Had it not

| FILE 62-098657 | CERTIFICATE OF DEATH STATE OF CALIFORNIA DEPARTMENT OF PUBLIC HEALTH | DISTRICT AND 7053 | 17716 |

Marilyn			Monroe		August 5, 1962	3 AM
Female	Cauc.	Los Angeles, Calif.	June 1, 1926	36		
unk.	unk.	Gladys Pearl Baker -Mexico	United States	5f 3-32-0756		
Actress	20	20th Century-Fox	Motion Pictures			
none		Divorced				

PLACE OF DEATH

	12305 -5th Helena Drive		
Los Angeles	Los Angeles	36	36

LAST USUAL RESIDENCE

12305 -5th Helena Drive	X		Mrs. Inez C. Melson
Los Angeles	Los Angeles	Calif.	9110 Sunset Blvd.

PHYSICIAN'S OR CORONER'S CERTIFICATION

autopsy		Theo J. Curphey M.D. Coroner
		HALL OF JUSTICE LOS ANGELES 8-28-62

FUNERAL DIRECTOR AND LOCAL REGISTRAR

Entombment	Aug.8,1962	Westwood Memorial Park	Charles Wayne
Westwood Village Mortuary	SEP 1 2 1962		Leona M. Weir, M.D.

CAUSE OF DEATH

ACUTE BARBITURATE POISONING

INGESTION OF OVERDOSE

MEDICAL AND HEALTH DATA

Probable Suicide   As Above

3A 8-5-62   Home   Los Angeles   LA   Calif.

A death that shocked and saddened the world. "Probable suicide?" Absolutely not.

been that way, Marilyn's body wouldn't have been discovered until 3:30 in the morning when her housekeeper arrived.

Where was Joe? That's the question I posed to my mother when I called. Just as I was asking her, Joe and my father walked in. They had been at the restaurant.

Joe immediately flew to Los Angeles to take over.

MOTHER TOLD ME that she *knew* who killed Marilyn, but that knowledge absolutely terrified her, and to protect us, she said that she would never reveal the details of what she knew.

Who did it? Who could have wanted the gloriously good-natured Marilyn Monroe dead? I will never know for sure, and I could not perceive it by ESP at all. When it comes to myself, I never have any perceptions, only for others.

I begged Mother to tell me who it was over and over and over again. She was not only traumatized but stubborn, the Swiss German in her rising to the surface.

Uncle Joe also pleaded with her to confide in him many times. No matter how many stories come out that Joe learned who killed Marilyn, they're not true. Only Mother knew, and she never confided in Joe or anyone else. He kept asking her, "Won't you tell me now, Lee? Won't you tell me now, Lee?" and she just said, "No, I want my family to live."

Nothing that I said was able to bend Mother's iron will once she had made up her mind that if we knew, we could be in danger.

Whoever killed her must have been very, very powerful to frighten my mother into everlasting silence. My smart, spunky mother was terrified to the very end and took the truth to her grave.

Even after the FBI traced that last call that Marilyn made to Mother, not even the country's G-men could make inroads with her. As she told me directly and in no uncertain terms, she wouldn't tell anything to the FBI or to another living soul.

Whenever we begged her, she would press her lips together and draw her fingers across them, to pantomime that she was zipping them tight. When I kept at her, she admitted her terror that if she told, "they" would kill her family.

Photographer Gene Anthony took this shot of Marilyn's kitchen through the apartment's French doors. It shows the Mexican tiles she'd bought and placed around the sink.

Uncle Joe still had good connections in the media and with law enforcement. He hushed up the fact that my mother had been on the phone with Marilyn when she died. He knew well that reporters would hound her, and he didn't want Mother to go through any more than she already had.

AND SO MARILYN'S memorial service took place on the very day she and Joe were to be remarried.

Instead of the joy he longed for, instead of preparing for the wedding to the love of his life, Joe made preparations for her funeral. Instead of the wedding day he had waited so long for, on August 8, 1962, he laid his beloved Marilyn Monroe to rest at Westwood Memorial.

I remember profound sadness in his eyes, and resignation too. He couldn't bear for Marilyn to be exploited yet again, and was adamant about keeping the media, the studio moguls, and the curious away from her funeral. The public had gawked at her long enough; he was determined to give her the privacy and dignity she had longed for all her career.

He made sure that the service was very private, yet Joe was surrounded that day by many people; some who were genuinely trying to comfort him, others who were just hanging onto his celebrity. I was there to pay my respects only briefly. I just couldn't bring myself to stay for the entire ceremony. I knew the casket would be open only for the family. I slipped in and said my good-byes to Marilyn privately and then made my way into the crowd at the cemetery.

I wanted to remember her as the young, vivacious, loving soul I had gotten to know so well over eleven years. I wanted to remember how her smile lit up a room, how she made me laugh about the most trivial things.

When I knew her, she was alive and filled with hope and dreams. She might go down in history as one of Hollywood's greatest stars, but I wanted to remember her as my dear friend. No one else in my family could bring themselves to attend Marilyn's service.

After all was said and done, Joe came to my place, where he knew he didn't have to meet and greet anyone. Joe needed time to just be himself and come to grips with his pain and suffering. As usual, he was stoic, enduring his sorrow in silence. I prepared a simple meal for him of leftover boiled beef, but he hardly touched a bite. None of us was hungry.

Barbara talked with him then about life and death. We both tried to be there for him, allowing him a safe place to grieve in private. He stayed for quite some time and then I drove him back to his hotel.

UNCLE JOE'S BALL-PLAYING days were long over, but he continued to love the game of baseball until his death. His baseball fame gave him an entrée into television commercials for Mr. Coffee and the Dime Savings Bank of Brooklyn. That exposure brought him recognition from a new generation, but I don't think he cared much about the fame. He made those commercials for the money.

After he retired as a player, he was hired as a coach and ambassador for the Oakland A's, but that lasted just a short time. He confided to us that while he may have been a great player, his greatness didn't extend to coaching.

We stayed in touch, and Barbara and I saw Joe at Thanksgiving and Christmas at the restaurant. Joe liked Barbara, and even consulted with her from his home in Florida when he was facing heart surgery, because she had had a four-bypass operation.

She told him that if he were afraid of the surgery, which he said he was, he would "defeat the purpose of the doctors and yourself."

"Do you have another alternative?" she asked.

"Yes, I could have a pacemaker," he answered.

"Then have that, if you have no fear," she said.

Joe did have the pacemaker inserted and lived quite a while afterward, dying ultimately of lung cancer.

Joking around at DiMaggio's one holiday, Joe turned to Barbara and said, "Will you marry me?" with a big smile on his face.

She turned to him with her own gorgeous smile and said, "But you don't play football, Joe."

In Memory of
Marilyn Monroe

Born
June 1st, 1926

Passed Away
August 5th, 1962

Services
Wednesday, August 8th, 1962
Westwood Memorial Park

Officiating
Reverend A. J. Soldan
Village Church of Westwood

Entombment
Westwood Memorial Park

Bok Singing Tower

What sadness my Uncle Joe felt to bury his true love on the very day they were to be remarried.

With solemn faces, the invited guests—with my Uncle Joe on the left in the second row—bid farewell to Marilyn at her crypt.

The press and spectators were kept at a distance when Marilyn was buried. Joe wanted her to be free of the crowds and onlookers, at least on this last day.

The crowd pushed against the fence to get a glimpse of the graveside service. According toto photographer Gene Anthony, moments after the invited guests departed, the souvenir-seeking fans took the funeral flowers and even branches and leaves from nearby trees.

Marilyn's swimming pool and patio. She never used it much herself, preferring to make it available to friends. Her robe is thrown over the chaise lounge where she left it the afternoon before her death.

We all had a big laugh over that little joke.

Joe's love for Marilyn lived on as well, and famously so. He never married again and for many years saw that there were fresh flowers at Marilyn's crypt. Visitors, however, stole the flowers again and again. After quite a lot of frustration, Joe gave up and stopped sending them.

When Joe was dying, he said to his attorney, "Now I'll be with my beautiful Marilyn."

Joe didn't send flowers to Marilyn at the end of his life, but he went to his grave loving her, I know.

June DiMaggio Epilogue

Although the public knew Marilyn as a fair-haired goddess of the silver screen, she was a woman; a human being, first and foremost.

Had she lived longer, had she been stronger, had times changed, her fans might have known her better as a remarkable woman. I'm sure that they would have loved her still, but in a deeper, more meaningful way.

I know that I loved Marilyn the person most, and I wish that she could have run up the stairs to my apartment for a laugh and lasagna for many more years.

Marilyn understood that it's not what you accomplish or how much money you make or the acclaim you receive, but what positive marks you make and leave behind that count.

That's why this book matters so much to me, and why I'm grateful that Barbara Klein and radio and television host Mary Jane Popp encouraged me to tell my story.

For all our years together, Barbara remained a counselor to me. Without her, I shudder to think how my retirement days would have gone. I got out of Hollywood before I became a has-been actress finding it impossible to get work or tempted to give in to the casting couch or letting untrustworthy hangers-on waste my money. Barbara wouldn't let that happen to me. Her Pennsylvania Dutch background grounded me and kept me conservative and frugal. I would get to enjoy the money I earned, but she made me put much of it away for that rainy day. To this day I'm grateful to Barbara for helping me with my finances.

When I did *Showboat* I made $5,000, and that was a helluva lot of money in those days.

"You keep a thousand to pay expenses, and with the rest you buy AT&T stock," Barbara said at the time. "It's called an 'old lady' stock and it will never go out of business." Every show I did, I put aside a third of what I earned and bought AT&T stock. Then, when AT&T became a conglomerate, she said, "Get out."

Early on Barbara taught me an important lesson, which I still use to this day: *Give advice only when people ask for it. Otherwise, they'll never accept it and use it properly.*

She offered investment insights, but gave actual advice only when I asked for it.

Barbie was never a complainer. She never whined, even though she suffered from myriad maladies. She always gave her all and put everyone's needs ahead of her own.

She wrote, she coached, she counseled—and she heeded the same advice she gave to others. I believe a great deal of her caring for her students came as a result of her spiritual grounding.

She was the most selfless person I have ever known, and knowing her has made all the difference.

I just know she's up there somewhere, encouraging me to tell it like it was.

Mary Jane Popp Epilogue

As a talk-show host and investigative reporter for more than thirty years in radio and television, I have come across many fascinating stories, but the one I am about to tell ranks at the top of my list.

I truly think that the universe was trying to tell me something, because the following account came long after I heard and wrote about Marilyn's last day from June. I always search for verification to stories, and this one piqued my curiosity.

It happened during an interview on my "POPPOFF" radio show in Sacramento, California. I have met the famous and the infamous in my years in the communication business—from Nancy Reagan to Mr. Blackwell—but this personality had intrigue written all over him, and the interview left me speechless.

Alan Kimble "Kim" Fahey met them all—murderers, psychos, perverts; even the stars that shine in Hollywood. From movie stars' homes and hangouts to hospitals, prisons, and morgues, Kim got to hear stories and to witness events that no one else ever could. Why? Kim worked as a telephone repairman in Los Angeles for Pacific Bell, Western Electric, AT&T, and Bell Labs. For thirty-five years he was the proverbial fly on the wall that no one noticed, and he kept his ears open and his mouth shut.

In his book, *Hollywood Unlisted,* he tells hair-raising stories of those exploits. After interviewing him on my radio show, we continued talking off the air, and I asked him if he had any stories about Marilyn Monroe.

Kim Fahey's story was incredible, but this telephone repairman had lots of tales to tell in his book, "Hollywood Unlisted." Mary Jane had an enlightening one-on-one visit with Kim at his home.

He did, and later related the story I'm about to share with you in a one-on-one interview in his kitchen in Acton, California.

As the tape recorder rolled, I was mesmerized. Kim's story certainly validated what June DiMaggio and I already knew; Marilyn Monroe was murdered.

The story took place around the early '80s, when Kim was sent to do about three days of phone work on a system at Atascadero State Mental Hospital, a maximum-security facility on California's central coast. Kim was minding his work, converting an old switchboard to a new phone system, when he was confronted by a thin, wiry man.

The Guy, as I will refer to him, was in his late fifties or early sixties, of medium build, maybe 145 pounds, with slicked-back, graying hair. Kim said that he spoke in a streetwise tone and seemed desperate to talk to someone.

During the next day or so, he talked with Kim as he worked. As the last day approached, the Guy said, "Take me to lunch and I'll tell you a good story." Kim decided it was worth a listen for a cheap lunch in the cafeteria. The following story emerged, and my eyes got bigger and bigger as it unfolded.

Kim didn't remember his name, but the Guy claimed that he and his partner had murdered Marilyn Monroe. He told Kim he was a small-timer in the Sam Giancana crime family in the East. The goal of anyone working for the mob was to move up in the family, so when he was told to go to California to do the deed he had no hesitation. He was told to shut Marilyn up and get a journal she had been keeping. The order was clear: Do whatever it takes, and do it quietly.

It seems that what she was writing in that journal was making some very powerful people nervous. The Guy had never been to Los Angeles and didn't know his way around, so a driver was provided for him and his partner. The driver, he said, never knew what they were about to do.

They stalked Marilyn for several days to find out her routines. They discovered that part of her nightly routine was to sedate herself a little, take a drink or two, and crash on the bed in her bedroom with the TV on.

During the time they stalked her, they also lifted her keys and had duplicates made of all of them, since they weren't sure which ones they would need. Finally they chose the night to make their move.

They let themselves in the front door. The Guy said they didn't see anyone else in the house. They entered her room and, as expected, found Marilyn in bed.

Before she could react, they were on top of her. Both men held her down while the Guy inserted a suppository (supplied for the purpose when they arrived in California) into her rectum. They had been told that it would work quickly and that it would not show up in an autopsy.

The Guy said that Marilyn struggled for only a minute or so, and then she stopped breathing. All was quiet. The search for the journal didn't take long; they found it under the mattress. They left in a matter of minutes, making sure that the front door was locked behind them and leaving no evidence of a break-in.

They turned the journal over to the driver, a member of Giancana's organization.

And that was the end of the story . . . or was it?

The Guy thought he was going to move up in the Giancana crime family because of his slick work, until he heard that his partner had been murdered and that there was a contract out for him, too. He knew that he had to do something drastic, and fast.

He'd never been outside New York or Chicago for any length of time and didn't want to leave the country, so he devised another plan. He stole someone's identification in order to bury his own.

He told Kim that he stole an ID that had a physical description close to his. He didn't want to be arrested and put in the general population in prison because he knew the mob could get to him from inside.

So he got a crazy idea to pretend that he was crazy. He got into an altercation in a restaurant, acted nutty, got arrested, and was subsequently admitted to Atascadero State Mental Hospital.

Crazy as the plan was, it might have worked. He may have thought that he could hide in the hospital and be released when things cooled off. What he didn't know was that the stolen ID was from a guy with a rap sheet longer than his arm who was a bona fide nut case.

Now the Guy is identified as and believed to be mentally ill and the authorities have locked him away forever at Atascadero.

He's in a bind because if he disputes his incarceration, he has to prove his real identity. Apparently he decided to accept his fate as a mental patient rather than the likely alternative fate of being whacked.

Is he still alive? Perhaps. Kim told me that he would probably know the Guy if he saw him again, but Kim never returned to the facility for another job. Even as he can recall the man's face, Kim said that the details of the Guy's story remain vivid in his memory. He believes that the Guy is either still incarcerated or that he's died. Blown away by the story and curious about why Marilyn was murdered, I asked more questions.

There have long been rumors about Frank Sinatra's involvement, but why would Sinatra, who cared deeply and remained a loyal friend to Marilyn, want her dead? How about the studio executives who tried to control Marilyn at all costs? For them to have a hand in killing her would be like shooting themselves in the pocketbook. You don't kill the cash cow.

Perhaps the most talked-about theory is that a high-level law enforcement agency, such as the FBI, had Marilyn killed, but a former military intelligence officer has said that the way it happened isn't the FBI's style. First, he said, the FBI doesn't kill people. Second, according to my source, the use of the suppository at that time was a method associated with and preferred by European and Russian assassins. That could point to the CIA, which often hired killers, but we don't know for sure.

Then there's the longtime theory tying the Kennedy family to the mob that dates back to the heyday of wealthy financier and family patriarch Joseph Kennedy, associating him with Gianana or "Momo," as he was called, *il capo di Chicago*.

Could it have been a diabolical plan by Momo to bring down Bobby Kennedy (rumored to have been Marilyn's lover, although June told me that Marilyn adamantly denied sleeping with him or his brother, Jack), as referenced in the book *Double Cross*, by sending in his two trusted thugs, "Needles" Gianola and "Mugsy" Tottorella? That theory says that they killed the star and made her death look like suicide while implicating Bobby Kennedy at the same time. Could one of those two thugs have been the man Kim talked with at Atascadero?

I remember interviewing Thomas Noguchi in 1984 after he published his book, *Coroner*. Noguchi, nicknamed "the coroner to the stars," was chief medical examiner of Los Angeles County and performed the autopsy on Marilyn. I asked him point-blank if he believed that Marilyn had been murdered. I remember that he hesitated and gave a pat answer, offering the same words written on her death certificate, "probable suicide." Noguchi may have been hedging his bet, but he, too, wrote that without the details of the FBI files disclosed to the public, no one will know for sure what happened that night when Marilyn was found, her hand on the telephone. And those files, I've been told, have mysteriously been destroyed.

And so it goes. Many questions surrounding the circumstances of Marilyn's death remain unanswered and intriguing forty-four years later. Clearly, the public has an enormous appetite for the story in life and death of this larger-than-life star. Theories abound, and the Internet offers a wealth of information and suppositions about what really happened. Former Los Angeles County prosecutor John Miner, now eighty-eight, has spoken again about reopening the investigation into her death and exhuming her body to reexamine it and reconsider the finding that she committed suicide.

What I do know after my investigative interviews and my long relationship with June is that Marilyn was murdered. I have no doubt.

It was our job to tell the truth—to tell it like it was—and we went to the source.

Only Marilyn, who would have celebrated her eightieth birthday this year, and Lee DiMaggio, who went to her grave trying to protect her family, know what really happened.

And they are painfully quiet.

APPENDIX

DiMaggio Family Recipes

CHICKEN LA CACCIATORE (HUNTER'S STYLE)

1 fresh chicken
16 oz. canned tomatoes or
    2 fresh (whole or chopped)
6 oz. can tomato paste
Rosemary
Oregano
Basil
8 oz. dry vermouth
Olive oil
8 oz. canned or fresh mushrooms

Prepared on stove top

Cut chicken into small pieces. Be sure to take off all fat. Place in large frying pan with olive oil, tomatoes, (fresh or canned) tomato paste, rosemary, oregano, and basil. Let simmer for 30 minutes. After half an hour add 8 oz. dry vermouth. Let simmer for just a few minutes more for flavor to settle. Add canned or fresh mushrooms.

20-MINUTE SPAGHETTI SAUCE

16 oz. canned tomatoes or
    2 fresh (whole or chopped)
Butter
Mushrooms
Parsley
Oregano
Basil
Rosemary
1 brown onion

This will be the fastest recipe for spaghetti sauce you ever made, but it is delicious. Just add two tomatoes or one can of tomatoes, enough butter to moisten the mixture, 8 oz. of sliced mushrooms, a touch of parsley, oregano, basil, rosemary, and one diced brown onion. Add water to desired texture and boil for 20 minutes. Salt and pepper optional.

ANNIE RUDIE'S RAVIOLI

RAVIOLI

Pre-prepared raviolis or your own
   favorite dough recipe
1 lean sirloin steak finely ground
   (powdered)
Parmesan cheese
Swiss chard
Calf brains—about one third the
   amount of the steak

SAUCE

16 oz. canned tomatoes or
   2 fresh (whole or chopped)
6 oz. tomato paste
Oregano
Basil
Persa (a mild, sweet herb)
Rosemary
Olive oil
Parmesan cheese
2 cloves finely chopped garlic

Roll out the dough and add a prepared mixture of sirloin steak, calf
brains, finely chopped Swiss chard
and Parmesan cheese to the dough.
Place another dough layer on top and
cut ravioli into extra large squares.
Place in boiling water until the raviolis are tender. Meanwhile, prepare
the sauce with fresh or canned tomatoes, tomato paste, a pinch of
oregano, basil, persa, rosemary, and a
touch of olive oil, Parmesan cheese,
and two finely chopped garlic cloves.
Simmer for about 20 minutes. Serve
the raviolis with this fabulous sauce.

   Recommendation: You don't
have to mention the brains, and your
guests will love the taste. And don't
mention to Annie Rudie that I
snitched her secret ingredient to you.

DIMAGGIOS' CLAM CHOWDER

½ pound clams (fresh or canned)
1 chopped brown onion or
   3 green onions (scallions), chopped
8 oz. creamed corn
Butter
Milk

In a pot add canned or fresh clams
along with the juice, one can of

creamed corn, and three or four green
onions finely chopped or chopped
brown onion if you prefer. Add
2 tablespoons butter and one glass
of milk. Simmer for 10–15 minutes.
If you desire a thicker texture, add
1 tablespoon of cornstarch to the
mixture.

DIMAGGIO'S SAVORY SQUID

Cut up squid parts (about 1 lb.)
Cornstarch
Butter
Olive oil

Roll squid parts in cornstarch until
completely covered. Deep fry in half
butter and half olive oil until golden
brown, and serve.

SUSPENSEFUL CHILI

1 lb. chili-grind hamburger
"Grandma's" Chili Powder brand
    name (not hot)
16 oz. diced tomatoes
16 oz. kidney beans
1 big chopped brown onion

In medium-sized pot, add hamburger and 2 heaping tablespoons "Grandma's" Chili powder. You may like more, because it is not hot and just adds flavor. Add diced tomatoes, kidney beans, and finely chopped brown onion. Simmer over low heat for about 25 minutes.

JOE'S BOILED BEEF

1–2 lbs. of beef short ribs
2 sticks celery
2 carrots
4 medium new potatoes
1 lb. ditalini (small pasta)
Parmesan cheese

In soup pot add short ribs and boil for 20 minutes. Add two sticks of coarsely chopped celery, two coarsely chopped carrots, and new potatoes. Boil for 20 minutes longer. Remove vegetables and cook ribs an additional 30 minutes. Add ½ lb. ditalini and simmer an additional 10 minutes. Serve the soup first with Parmesan topping. Then serve the meat and the vegetables together as the main entree.

JOE'S WHIMSICAL WILD DUCK

1 wild duck
1 medium sliced brown onion
1 stick celery cut into
    ½-inch thick sticks
1 sliced apple

Preheat oven to 350 degrees.

Stuff the wild duck with sliced onion, celery, and sliced apple. Bake Teal duck for 30 minutes. Bake Mammoth for 40–45 minutes. Serve with plain wild rice (butter optional).

DIMAGGIO'S CIOPPINO

1 lb. clams
1 lb. crab
1 lb. shrimp
1 lb. halibut
16 oz. canned tomatoes or
    2 fresh tomatoes

Preheat oven to 250 degrees.
    In a casserole combine clams, shredded crabmeat, shrimp, and shredded halibut. Add tomatoes and bake for 30 minutes.

MARILYN'S TERRIFIC LOBSTER THERMADOR

1 lb. lobster, shelled
Butter
Beer
Tillamook cheese

Remove lobster from shell. Butter the inside of the shell. Meanwhile, marinate the lobster in beer for one hour. Place lobster back in the shell and cover with Tillamook cheese. Broil for 5–10 minutes. The beer is the key to delicious!

MARILYN'S LUSCIOUS LASAGNA

1 lb. large pasta
1 lb. ground sirloin
2 tomatoes
6 oz. tomato paste
Parmesan cheese
Rosemary, oregano, basil to taste
One clove garlic, finely chopped
One brown onion
Mozzarella cheese slices

Preheat oven to 350 degrees.
    Boil the pasta for three minutes until pliable. Cut in 3-inch squares and layer casserole.

Cook sauce made with hamburger, tomatoes, tomato paste, Parmesan cheese, rosemary, oregano, basil, and garlic for 20 minutes. Spoon sauce on the layered pasta, then layer with slices of Mozzarella cheese. Cover the sauce with an additional layer of pasta. Make four layers. Cut into 3-inch squares. Bake for 20–25 minutes.

ITALIAN THROAT REMEDY FOR LARYNGITIS AND SORE THROAT

5 ounces of water
4 full tablespoons of red wine vinegar
    (must be red wine vinegar,
    no other)
1 heaping tablespoon of salt

Mix in a glass or jar and gargle several times a day until throat is better. This concoction helps to soothe sore throats and helps laryngitis to make a fast exit, too.

INCREDIBLE ITALIAN RUM CAKE

3 egg yolks
¾ cup sour cream
1 cup granulated sugar
1 teaspoon vanilla extract
2¼ cups all-purpose flour
½ teaspoon nutmeg
¼ teaspoon salt
1 cup butter
½ cup dark rum
4 eggs
2 cups milk
¼ teaspoon baking soda
½ lemon peel, grated
¾ cup chopped coconut

Preheat oven to 350 degrees.

Beat the yolks and ¼ cup of the sugar in a mixing bowl and slowly add ¼ cup of the flour. Meanwhile, place the milk in a small pot and bring to the brink of boiling. Slowly pour the milk over the yolk mixture, then pour everything back into the pot. Place over medium heat and cook, stirring constantly until it thickens. Remove from heat and mix in the lemon peel. Spoon into a plastic container, cover, and place in refrigerator to chill.

At high speed in your mixer, cream the butter and remaining sugar.

Add the eggs one at a time, waiting for each to be absorbed before adding the next. Add the sour cream and mix until incorporated. Add vanilla extract, nutmeg, baking soda, coconut, and salt. Decrease the speed to medium, add remaining flour, and mix another minute or so. Scrape the batter into a 1-quart round or rectangular cake pan, leaving about 1 inch at the top. Place on the middle rack of the oven for 50–60 minutes. The cake is done when the surface cracks and a wooden toothpick inserted into the center comes out clean.

Remove the cake from the oven and let cool for 15 minutes before unmolding from pan. When the cake is completely cool, slice it into six layers. Place the first layer on a cake platter and sprinkle with some of the rum. Cover the layer with some of the custard mixture. Place the second layer on top of the custard, sprinkle with rum and cover with more custard. Continue until the cake is assembled. Lightly spread the custard all over the surface of the cake. Refrigerate at least 2 hours before serving. I think Mother's addition of the coconut made it incredible!

JEANETTE MACDONALD'S LEMON BISQUE

13 oz. evaporated milk
1 pkg. lemon-flavored gelatin
1¼ cups boiling water
Grated rind of 1 lemon
⅛ teaspoons salt
3 tablespoons lemon juice
⅓ cup honey
2 cups crushed vanilla wafers

Chill milk in refrigerator overnight. Dissolve gelatin in boiling water and add honey, salt, lemon juice, and rind. When it has congealed slightly, beat evaporated milk until stiff and whip gelatin mixture into it. Spread half of the crumbs in pan and pour lemon mixture atop. Top with remaining crumbs and set in refrigerator to chill overnight. May be served with whipped cream. Serves twelve.